His Guidance through Life's Storms:

Mark's journey from addiction to salvation, and selling pills to prints

2nd edition - October 2019

Table of Contents

Introduction

I go into detail about some of the things of my past in the beginning of this book. I do not do this to glorify anything I have done, but rather, to give you an inside perspective into my life. My story is like many others in our society who get tangled up with twisted logic to justify their ends, but this story is solely mine. My purpose is so you know that I have a past of addiction, but that Jesus has saved me from it and given me a future. Knowing where I have come from and where Jesus found me gives me that much more reassurance that God has a plan for my life. I was not a good person, and am still *very* far from perfect. There is no good in me except through Jesus. Some people put me on a pedestal after the coverage of "Life In The River". It is not necessary. I owe my life and all my talents to the Lord, who saved me from my demons. All I am, all that I do, is because of His blessings in my life.

The story is mine, but the names of those involved in my past life have been changed.

I want to thank my family and loving wife Kristin, for putting up with me through all the years, along with my friends who stuck by my side and supported me however possible. A special thanks to Steve Clifton, Robert Tebbs, Stephen Kelley, Matt Bluejay, Steve McCoy, Steve Schnell, Kevin Akers, Kate Hallock, Windi Wellence, Michele Luthin, Lindsay Powell, Jen Jones, Catherine Lee, and last but not least Brooks and JR Holland. My story has been dramatically impacted by all of these people's love and support in one way or another, and I deeply appreciate all they do.

1. Early Life

My first memory is in one of our bathrooms in Richmond, TX. There was a sign, with a big orange cat pawing at toilet paper, which said "Let the good times roll!". I grew up in a middle class family, and by all accounts had a happy upbringing in Richmond. I was the only child in our immediate family, with one cousin in Houston. Building bamboo forts, playing super Nintendo, riding bikes, and going to county fairs were a regular thing to me. Boy scouts, soccer teams, just hanging out being a kid. Riding the bus to school past fields of Bluebonnets and Indian Paintbrushes in the spring was what I grew up with. Listening to George Strait playing on the radio on my hour long rides to and from school, which was located in Fulshear, TX. The closest (and best) BBQ restaurant around was The Swinging Door, which would clear out their back hall of chairs on Friday night for square dancing. I will always be that boy from Texas in my heart.

My mother was active in the Huggins Elementary PTA, and was the president for several years. She would get my whole school grade cookies for Christmas parties from three brothers bakery. They had the best cookies around! I was in boy scouts, and was a top salesman of boy scout fair tickets. I won several trophies, for outstanding salesman. Those trophies were almost as big as I was. I really enjoyed the prizes I could win if I applied myself, and had that drive. Although twice in my aggressive door to door sales tactics I got bit by dogs, it was still a wonderful

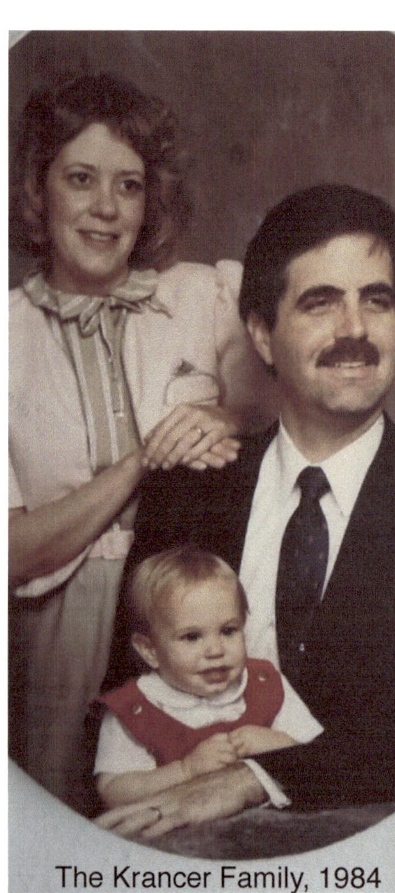

The Krancer Family, 1984

experience. Being able to earn a bike or a tent, some of the bigger prizes, was pretty cool!When I was 7, I wrote in a school assignment that I wanted to grow up to sell things. I forgot all about this until I stumbled on it as a 32 year old man.

My mom and I would often take the hour long drive to Galveston or Surfside and search for seashells along the beach. Looking for shells was one of our favorite activities together. Of course, I regularly went swimming in the ocean as well.

My mom ran for the school board, with the slogan "Krancer is the Answer." She lost to a gentlemen named Bill Head, whose campaign signs simply said "Head" in capital purple letters on a white background. After that, she never ran again, but continued to stay active in the school.

In 1996, my parents divorced. My father had cheated on my mother with a black woman. This was something that, when my peers found out, I would occasionally get teased about. I never really felt remorse or guilt about it. I used my mom's guilt about it as a way to just do what I wanted. When we moved to the neighborhood of First Colony in Sugarland, TX, I lacked ambition to do anything, and thought I knew it all. And I could get away with quite a bit.

In 1997, my father and I went with our boy scout troop to Philmont, New Mexico. Hiking with our backpacks containing our needs for two weeks, and continually moving our camp, gave me an appreciation of the beauty in nature. The stars from the mountains were truly awe inspiring. There was no light pollution anywhere around, and they were incredibly bright. They almost force you to notice them.

I had a Kodak disposable camera, as well as a panoramic disposable camera. I took photos of the beautiful mountain ranges along our journey. I also learned a valuable lesson about shooting safely when I almost blew my foot off while attempting to shoot clay pigeons. The instructor asked if I had my finger off the trigger, and I was so excited to shoot that I told him "yes". He loaded the barrel, and instantly the shotgun went off, just a few inches from my feet. That definitely shocked me, and embarrassed me in front of the entire troop. I cried to my dad that day, pretty badly.

My time in the boy scouts was waning, however. We had moved, so we were physically disconnected from the troop, and my new friends were becoming more interesting to hang out with. We would bike around and smoke cigarettes and be so cool in our eyes. Sometimes we would go workout, and then have Popeye's fried chicken as our post workout meal. We would hunt snakes by the lake, kill them and skin them up along the fence line. I was just another knucklehead kid with no direction and no consideration for others. We did dumb things, like throw a bunch of rocks in our neighbors pool. Then the police got called, and we all got a good lecturing at my house. We got off lucky! Ironically, we had a similar situation happen with our boys and their friends with a neighbor recently. I guess it seems like a good idea at the time to kids.

2. Life is all about Choices

I tell my stepsons, Gavin and Logan, that life is all about choices. Looking back, I can see how choices I made at 13 followed me for years to come. I liked money, and I enjoyed selling things. Ultimately, these choices put me on the trajectory I am on today. In middle school, I sold icebreakers gum that I bought at Randall's grocery store and then sold in class. 25 cents a piece. I had a small business that gave me something to do, and a couple extra bucks in my pocket a day.

I had smoked my first cigarette out of my mom's pack of Benson and Hedges ultra light 100's at age 12. Soon after that, we would get ahold of packs of black and mild cigars, and between a friend and myself inhale a whole black and mild. We would be so high from the nicotine that we could not move for at least 30 minutes afterwards, so we would often times just lay down at the lake by my house. Around the time I came back from Philmont, my good buddy William and I tried weed for the first time together in a treehouse out behind my neighborhood. I felt a connection to nature, being high up in the treehouse, and high at the same time. That euphoric state, and disconnect from life, was what I enjoyed.

I have an addictive personality. Whether it is food (I was a fat kid growing up), or games, or drugs, once I find something I really enjoy, I become addicted to the point of it becoming unhealthy. This was particularly true with an online game called Everquest. I played as a bard (first level 60 bard on the Cazic-Thule server) and was a guild leader. But my obsession with the game lead me to spend nights playing until 4 or 5am on a school day. One time, I camped out for an item (a Rubicite breastplate) for 30 hours straight. Once I could sell my stuff on Ebay, the financial part of it came in. I made a few thousand dollars selling things online. When I finally quit the game in 2001, and started smoking much more weed, all my grades improved dramatically because I was not just sleeping through class any longer.

Ultimately, my experience selling products in the past ended up easily transferring to drugs. It starts simply enough. Buy an ounce of regs for $40, sell 2 "20 sacks" (10 grams each), and get 8 grams for yourself so you can smoke for free. Eventually demand increases, and I would seek more supply. I decided I could also sell weed at school quietly, by selling weed brownies. In high school, I was baking a batch of brownies 3 to 5 times a week for school, where I could sell a brownie for 5 dollars, and make 60 dollars profit a day, and be high all through high school. Eating weed is very different from smoking it, it lasts much longer and the high is more mellow. So I just kept doing what I was doing, it seemed like a good thing. By 16, we were dabbling in cocaine, ecstasy, and basically anything else we could get our hands on, except for crack and heroine. Those drugs were bad, okay?

I had a few little legitimate jobs. I cleaned a bagel store for about 2 weeks. I worked at Chick-Fil-A for about a month, and Krogers grocery store for about 6 months. But I didn't really care about any of them, I didn't like working for companies. Why work when I can be my own boss and have a good time doing it? Oh, and make more money than working some lame job too! I quit Krogers when I decided to leave and go down to Crystal Beach near Galveston for a rave party instead of finish my shift. I ended up getting my 97 Chevy Cavalier stuck in the sand, and had to get pulled out by a hummer. Fun times, all while rolling on ecstasy!

I had a few encounters with jack boys. People always trying to get one over on you, especially in that world. But I could always bounce back through hustling. I would put in my work. There was no shortage of demand in my circle of friends. We all partied, we usually had keg parties somewhere on the weekend, and we all were up to no good. It's just how it was. We had gone car hopping one day when we were 16. Just checking for unlocked cars. We got a few things, including a fake ID that vaguely resembled me. I then used it to buy cigarettes and liquor at certain liquor stores. It was always a party then.

In 2001, our family moved to Dallas because my mother's job transferred there. It was the summer, and I was approaching my senior year in high school. We moved to Timberleaf, right off of 635 and Abrams in the heart of Dallas. I still sold brownies, and skipped school as often as I could. The new school was nothing compared to Clements, my old high school , educationally. Clements was one of the top public schools in Texas, while Lake Highlands HS was not. So I could really slide by like it was nothing and still keep my grades ok. It was early on in the school year at that new school that September 11th happened. That was a tragic time for the nation, and I remember it like yesterday. The initial confusion in our 1st period class, and then being in our 2nd period english class and watching live when the second plane hit. There was no confusion then what was going on, America was under attack. I didn't have some great surge of patriotism wash over me and want to join the army or anything, but I knew that the world as we all knew it was about to change very quickly.

 During this time frame, I got a new crew to ride around with and go car hopping. We would ride around and steal whatever we could from unlocked cars, and either trade directly to dealers for cocaine, or sell it at pawn shops. The night I graduated high school, this caught up with me and my buddy Joseph in a major way.

I was driving my car, a 97 chevy cavalier, while Joseph went into a car. Joseph found 2 cases of CDs, and a 500 watt amp, and started pulling them out the car. Another vehicle started to approach us, as Joseph came back into my car. I pulled away, drove a few streets, and parked in front of a house, acting like I was getting out to go into the house. The other car pulled up next to us, and asked what we were doing. They shouted "thats f*$#@ed up, you breaking into cars" and all this other stuff. I acted like I was replying, then I took off in the Cavalier as fast as I could.

I drove as best as I could, as evasively as possible in an attempt to lose these guys. But no matter what last minute turn I made, they followed. I was not going a crazy speed, as I did not want the cops to become involved. Eventually, I got on the interstate. It was about 2am by now, and there were not a lot of cars on the road besides us. I heard gunshots, and I told Joseph that it was just fireworks because I didn't want him to freak out on me. A few minutes later, they pulled up right next to us, rolled down the window, and out came a gun. I told Joseph "DUCK!!!" and not a second after I slammed on the breaks, the passenger of the Ultima was shooting at us. Fortunately, neither of us or the car was hit because I slammed on the brakes at the right moment.

Once the decision to shoot us had been made, my thought process took a different turn. Instead of evasion, I was ready to turn myself in to the cops. It was better to be locked up than dead. I did not have a gun, and I felt I had no other choice really. Joseph and I began heading towards a Dallas police station I knew of, next to a military base. I took the first entrance into the police station, and for the first time, our chasers did not immediately follow.

I turned off my headlights in the parking lot, and parked. I waited to see what they were doing, as they were across on the other side of the parking lot at the next entrance. When I knew they were heading the other way looking for us, I pulled out, with my headlights off, and went the wrong way down a one way street. In front of a police station. I then made my immediate left, which was a dead end into the military base.

I was surrounded by razor wire, a couple hundred yard road, and one streetlight. I knew at that point, if the Ultima with the gunmen came behind us, we were screwed. I stopped there, just out of the streetlight's direct light. Joseph and I prayed.

Neither of us were Christians, but still, we prayed for God to save us that night. He must have been listening, because I never saw the car or our attackers again.

I told my mom the next morning, as she was up by the time I arrived home. She didn't scorn me or really judge, she was just glad I was ok. I told myself I would never steal from another person, and I never have since. A few weeks later, I moved to Houston to start my illustrious college career at University of Houston. Those troubled times in Dallas were behind me. Little did I know more trouble awaited ahead.

Back in Houston, I was in trouble before school even started. That summer, once moved into the University of Houston dorms, I got busted with a bottle of liquor in my fridge. Not a good start as an 18 year old. I had the room advisor for the floor on me the rest of the time I was there.

A month later, I drove to see my old buddies at a house party in Missouri City, Texas. I had a bottle of Xanax that I needed to sell, and I sold about fifty of them. Mix alcohol and Xanax together, they enhance the effects of one another, so people become more violent. Combined with the alcohol, the party atmosphere began to change. A fight broke out between two people because of their nonsense and everyone started to leave. I was parked in the driveway, and the girl whose car was in front of me wanted to leave. I went to my car and put my beer in the cup holder. As soon as I put the car in reverse a police officer walked up to my car. He shined his light into my vehicle and saw my beer. He told me to park my car, while my buddy William was in the car with me. The cops went into the party to investigate the fight. We were drunk and "barred up" on Xanax. We thought this is our chance and I hit the gas full force. We approached a field, where I told William to toss the bottle of Xanax as far as he could. I drove a little bit after making a few turns and I saw the police lights again.

I was not going to run from the police when I knew they were chasing me. So I decided to stop. The cop pulled in front of me, screaming, "Why did you leave!??!" I replied, "I thought you told me I could go!" The cop made me drive in reverse all the way back to the house. I was incredibly drunk, barred up, and terrified. Despite the cop lights that were blindingly apparent in front of me, I did a good driving in reverse through the dark. Until the very end where I hit a parked car.

With the alarm blaring the cop arrested me for DWI or driving while intoxicated. It was my first trip to jail. My parents bailed me out the next day, and I was amazed to find my glass weed pipe sitting in plain view on the passenger side of the car. The cops never even searched the vehicle! My friend and I could have probably avoided a lot of that headache of trying to run from the cops. In hindsight, it would only prolong the path of destruction I was on.

My parents ended up taking my car away from me. However, it had no effect on my addiction. As a college student I was high on any drugs I wanted, partied whenever I could and made about $100 a day extra while middle manning and doing low-level drug deals. With all of this going on in the background, I was still able to do okay in school, but I was by no means a stellar student. One of the major drugs on campus was Adderall, so students could study for their tests. I always had a good supply of those on hand for my tests and to sell.

My roommate was a dork and to be fair I was a terrible roommate. I got drunk one night and even urinated all over his bed. I smoked weed in the room, did drug deals and had all sorts of people in the dorm room. After about a year he had had enough. In May, he told campus security where I kept my stash, as he had seen me using that spot. Campus security found me with a few Adderall pills and an "eighth" (about 3.5 grams) of marijuana. They gave me a choice either to leave the dorms and finish up the school year off of campus or face criminal charges for "possession of methamphetamine". I choose the lesser of the two evils which was to leave the dorms.

Living back at my dad's house was no picnic. He wasn't happy with me understandably so. He saw that my heart had not changed. To me, everyone was against me and I was just fine doing my own thing. After that semester ended my dad packed me with all of my stuff up. He sent me where my mom and grandma lived at the time, Palm Bay, Florida. My biggest concern was that I only had one ounce of weed to last me until I found a new connect in Florida.

I remember when I moved to Florida, I immediately noticed that the sky was a deeper blue than when I lived in Texas. Given my deep love for all things Texas, that is quite a statement for me. I went to the beach regularly with my mom and had a wonderful time searching for seashells with her like I did when I was a boy. It was nice to be back connected with family as well. My Uncle Ray lived down in West Palm Beach, and I always enjoyed his company. He had been in the drug scene for most of his adult life.

I started working once I moved to Palm Bay within a month. I got pretty lucky, with a job at Irwin research. It was an outbound customer service job which basically entailed calling random people in hopes that they would answer a survey. I could walk to my new job which made life much more simple.

Soon enough I started to meet people who partied. It was at a party after work that I met someone who would become my best friend, Carl. There was a fight at the party, and the cops were called so he decided to give me a ride home. Unbeknownst to me, they had taken the car that we were riding in from his mom and she had reported it stolen. This was a bad omen for our growing friendship. Little did I know how much of an influence we would have on each other lives over the next decade.

When the summer of 2003 was over, I started school at Brevard Community College while working full-time. I did well in school and I even made the President's list and became the top of my class in Biology, Macroeconomics, Microeconomics, and Oceanography. I wanted to be a lawyer specializing in criminal defense. I turned down an economics scholarship because Law was what I wanted to pursue. I got accepted to the University of Florida my junior year and toured the campus. In between school and work, my selling lifestyle came back around full force because in order to support my habit I had to sell. I was also addicted to the thrill of it all, the "game" of selling.

In March 2004 I walked up to work just like it was any other work day. Normally everyone hung around outside the building until our shift started. People noticed that there was a lock on the door and a sign that said, "The office has closed. Your paychecks will be in the mail." Surprisingly enough, I am still waiting on that paycheck to this day! Thankfully we were able to sign up for unemployment. I did not have any serious bills and I could generate a little money to live on from my drug dealing.

My 20th birthday party involved lots of LSD and Ecstasy which is commonly called "candy flipping". Of course we had cocaine, which I acquired from my new connection Max. He had quality product at a fair price, and was on time with delivery. We begin partying at a friend's house, and Carl inhaled some fumes from an air duster can. He began talking in demonic tones about the end of the world where demons will take over. Huffing air duster can give people a powerful but short-lived high. He later had a full-blown seizure. We were all too messed up to really do anything about it or get help. The only thing we were able to do was freak out. Those memories still haunt me.

Shortly after my 20th birthday my best friend from Houston, William, came to visit me in Florida on the date 4/20. For those who don't know, 420 is the international stoner holiday. Just an excuse to get extra high. I was preparing for 420 for many months by concocting a batch of green dragon, which is a marijuana infused alcoholic drink. For his 5 day stay we had 4 different types of marijuana, multiple bottles of liquor, LSD, ecstasy, cocaine, methadone, somas, Xanax, and Loritabs. I had been saving up for this time for months because William was a good friend and I wanted to celebrate as much as we could. We went to universal studios with friends where we dropped acid and had a blast.

We didn't remember much of 420 because we were so stoned on the various drugs we used. The brownies we baked that week were laced thick with weed and were extremely intoxicating. The last day William was in town we spent our time with my mother, who was a big influence in both of our lives back in Texas. We went to the beach and ate at one of my mom's favorite restaurants in Florida called the Shack which served seafood.

The vacation was ending as I had finals the next week and Carl had an early flight the next morning. We started the drive to the airport about 4:45 in the morning. William was leaving, so I gave him the honor of sitting shotgun. I sat in the back and we started heading northbound on 95 towards Orlando.

At mile 189 on Interstate-95 we heard a BANG! BANG! BANG! BANG! The sound was so loud and intense it caused us to hear it before we were able to see it. A white mass of metal that appeared to be an SUV was hurling through the air toward us. It was quickly flying through the lanes while flipping all around in our direction. My mom said ,"OH MY GOD" and she swerved towards the right in hopes to avoid this dangerous metal mass. Unfortunately, the oncoming danger was impossible to avoid. The SUV landed directly on top of my mother before continuing to flip down the road.

For years my mom had a bad habit of falling asleep while reading. Back then I would stay up pretty late. Before I would go to sleep, I would go into her room and take her glasses off of her face, then mark the page in the book that she was reading and turn her light off. She would fall asleep in the same position every night, with her chin down.

When the accident happened I instinctively ducked for cover. I wore glasses at the time and they flew off of my face with the force of the crash. William managed to get the car into the ditch in the median of Interstate-95. I found my mom's cell phone and called 911. In the dark pre-dawn hours of the day I ran around and opened my mom's car door. I got very close to her because I couldn't see her face clearly.

She looked exactly like she did on those frequent nights when she would fall asleep reading. Her chin was down and her eyes were closed. The only difference being there was no book that she was reading and she was covered in blood.

The 911 operator told me to apply pressure to the wound that I found on the top of her head. As I applied pressure, her skull was fractured in so many places that my hand sunk into her head as though it was mush.

No son should ever have that experience.

The fireman who came to the scene pulled me away and told me that she was dead. I called my grandma who lived with us at the time and I had to be the one to tell her that her oldest daughter, Roxanne, was dead. She screamed and wailed like I had never quite heard before. It brings tears to my eyes just reminiscing on it.

I was taken to the hospital where I was later released with just a few minor injuries. William survived the accident with only a broken nose. The next day my Uncle Ray and I drove William back down that same road to the airport. Needless to say I was a nervous wreck on that drive. Going on the exact same drive that killed my mother 24 hours earlier was gut wrenching. But we managed to get William on the plane, and my uncle Ray and I went home and did some cocaine.

Finals were on the calendar at Brevard Community College that week, after a few days of reviewing. Things were different this time as we no longer had a family car. I made the four mile walk to campus with sorrow in my heart at the deep loss I suffered.

I accomplished an A in every class and with some having over an 100 percent average because of extra credit. For 4 of my 5 classes, I just had to share the *FLORIDA TODAY* newspaper article stating what had happened with my mom. Once they saw the article, and given my grades thus far, I was excused from the finals. Professor Sohn, my oceanography professor, insisted that I stayed in the class despite what happened. This class I always participated in was one of my favorites. After the recent death of my mother I was in no mental state to be there. I stared blankly at the screen as the professor reviewed with the class. Professor Sohn asked me a question when I was zoning out. Once he got my attention, I said, "I don't know". At that point, he brought me out into the hallway to speak with him. He said I did not need to stay for the final and that he would take care of my grade. I thanked him, and I went home to take care of all of the other chaos in my life.

At the time of my mom's death I had just turned twenty. I didn't have a job and had very little unemployment money coming in. We rented our house that we all lived in and the family car had just been totaled in the accident. I had a drug habit and years of experience selling drugs. Therefore I chose the easiest route at the time: sell cocaine and pretty much anything else people asked for. I had no immediate financial sources to pay the bills otherwise and the insurance from the accident would take a few months to process. Life doesn't just stop, even if your life stops.

My Dad and step-mom Diana came down for the funeral where there was a bunch of people who loved my mom but I didn't have a chance to know. These people I didn't know sent their condolences and in a way that always bothered me. I think it's just a personal thing and part of my grieving process. Wanting to be alone combined with a drug habit can be a very terrible way to grieve.

I did not care about anything after my mom died. I popped Xanax by the handful. I remember at one point I had 500 Xanax pills, and I just took handfuls at a time, combined with liquor and somas and weed. Thankfully my buddy Carl was with me during this time. While estimates are unclear due to our severe inebriation during this period, we estimated that I took roughly 75 2 mg Xanax bars over a three day period. I completely blacked out. I woke up on a Sunday swearing to God it was a Thursday. My grandma started to wonder why I didn't come out of my room for at least two days.

My grandma had enough of me. I was selling drugs from the house that she was living in with me while bringing all sorts of people over to party. She was trying to rest and live the rest of her life however she could manage after losing her daughter. It was no place for her and she ended up moving in with my Aunt Lisa back in Houston. That was fine with me as I knew that I was on a dark path and I didn't care for her to get in my way. I know this was selfish thinking but that is exactly how I felt at the time. I saw her one more time in Houston before she passed away as well followed my Aunt Lisa passing shortly afterwards. My priorities were all in the wrong places, and I simply didn't have the desire to change.

3. Max Payne

I managed to take one little class at Brevard Community College to finish up my AA degree; physical education. That, I could handle mentally. Anything else and I seriously doubt I would have finished school. I was already accepted to University of Florida for the fall, but I postponed it. I was so wrapped up in the drug game, the easy money, the constant partying. It was a wonderful distraction where I did not have to focus on life. I could pay the bills, get high all I wanted, and not worry about a thing.

We had a regular crew of dealers who hung out at my house. Burt, Ralph, and Max were the inner circle of hustlers on our team. Max had the primary connection and re-up to replenish our supply in Miami. He could also be the muscle when the situation called for it. He had no hesitation about pulling a gun on someone the moment that drama started. I remember one time an addict who hadn't been around in a while showed up at the door, unannounced. They said they needed a jump for their car battery. I looked at Max, and he sprang up from his chair and line of cocaine, puts a gun in their face, and says "here is your jump!" They ran off quickly, and didn't get their jump. When we were collectively serving several hundred addicts and dealers on a regular basis drama was sure to come. Max's ride had a few bullet holes, people got tied up, and all sorts of other nonsense. I always tried to avoid that sort of thing as much as possible in my business. My way of avoiding that drama was ignoring it and pretending it didn't happen. I believed that it was generally bad for business and put a target on your back with law enforcement.

My insurance money eventually came through and I was able to buy a brand new 2004 Subaru legacy. I used a bit of the leftover money as an investment in the next level of the cocaine selling game. I was already selling an ounce of cocaine a day and now I was buying an eighth of a kilo which is 4.5

ounces. The supply and demand was so high that I was going through it rather quickly. To celebrate this elevation to such a status I naturally had to party harder than I ever did before. I took this block of cocaine and cut what I can only describe to someone as a slice of bread off of it. When I did that the "fish scales" glistened. Fish scales is when very high-quality cocaine is cut usually right off the key. I sat in this room with one of the dealers that I sold to and two girls. I got the Godfather book and made lines from side to side an inch high. I told them all that whoever could finish the line would get it for free. Naturally the dealer Paul rose to the occasion. I had to do it in three lines myself and I ended up just letting the girls have their fun. What a party, right?

Hurricane Frances just a few months after my mom had died. I had no real responsibilities but plenty of drugs and money. I loaded up my car with all my family belongings that I truly found valuable and just drove for an adventure. The day I was leaving, my Associates diploma came in the mail. No party, no celebration, no big walk, just the paper. At that point a piece of paper had no meaning because I didn't have my mom to share it with. I had my black fishing tackle box full of drugs consisting of two ounces of high grade coke, a quarter pound of weed, plenty of Xanax, Loritabs, Adderall, Somas, Trazadone, and a willingness to go hide out and pass the storm.

I was stuck in horrible traffic trying to leave town and I passed through this town called Jacksonville, Florida. I didn't know anything about the town and I kind of considered Jacksonville to be the armpit of Florida. It wasn't the glitz and glamour of south Florida or the picture I had of the state in my mind. As I crawled along Interstate-95 heading north where it took twelve hours to hit the state line, I had the time to look over and see downtown Jacksonville. It was beautifully placed along the river. This roundtrip was my only time going through Jacksonville for the next decade.

After eighteen hours of driving, I made my way to Walterboro, South Carolina. I had no ties to Walterboro but I figured it was a good a place to stop as any that was out of the storm's path. I would eat at the waffle house and eventually made the acquaintance of a brother and sister who happened to like the coke I had. After selling them eight balls (an eight ball is slang for an eighth of an ounce, 3.5 grams) and hanging out they invited me to their house for a home cooked meal. I had been eating out of gas stations and waffle house for days so the thought of a home cooked meal sounded good to me. I followed them way out in the country. This was before GPS and google maps made traveling much easier. I had no idea where I was but we ended up at their family's trailer miles away. Out came countless kids running around all dirty in true country fashion. I stayed with them for dinner and they made the best shepherd's pie I have ever had in my life. It was so wholesome and satisfying that I can still taste it today.

After stuffing my face with shepherd's pie we were hanging out with their parents in the living room. The parents gathered all the kids around and made a circle in the living room. I saw something that I figured was straight out of the twilight zone, they sat around listening to the radio. Something similar to *The Mask of Zorro* was playing which I thought that had stopped playing during the 1930s, but boy was I wrong! They did not get TV that far out in the country so they were forced to listen to the radio. After this culture shock, I went back to my hotel room and hung out with some meth head roofers selling them eight balls and doing rails. I watched the hurricane veer away from Palm Bay enough to not be a direct hit and then I went about on my merry way.

Eventually, I decided to get a job at a call center so I could try and look legit. On my 15 minute breaks I would run over to my buddy's house right across the tracks and do a couple rails of coke. Sometimes I would meet up with my more demanding clients too. This one pimp brought all his ladies to me and they each had their own quirks and tastes when it comes to drugs.

One woman would not do cocaine, but loved Adderall. If I could not get her Adderall, she would cry hysterically. In a fifteen minute break I could make a few sales over at this house across the tracks, get high, and make more money than I would in eight hours working at the call center. Although I kept the job to appear legit, my heart was following the dollars.

When I would work my cubicle job I would put my cell phone on call forwarding. Ryan was staying at my house but instead of paying rent he would just sell my drugs while I was at work. He could make me $500 profit while I just sat back at work. However a lot of people did not like dealing with him therefore when got I off at six in the evening, at 6:01pm my phone would explode. There would be four or five calls coming in within five minutes where everyone needed the product immediately. I would have one call come in and then put them on hold for another call. As soon as one deal was done I had to put someone else back on hold because of the call volume. I would not get a chance to do anything other than go slang after work. It worked out well because I could just do my drugs along the way. No matter the time of day, whether it was before work, during work, or after, I was always high in multiple ways.

Life was good in my eyes. I was making money and I was getting all the drugs I was capable of doing while everyone wanted to be my best buddy. My family was leaving me alone except my uncle Ray who was coming to me for his powder. I could party all I wanted to. I could have a half a dozen people lined up in their cars outside, and just walk down each and serve them. I tried not to do it that often because it caused a lot of attention, but there was just such demand on me and I had to be efficient. This drive-thru approach was labeled "MarkDonalds" by some of my people, but it was an easy way to make $300 in ten minutes. But what goes up, must come down.

We all did a lot of cocaine and stayed up very late. Sometimes I would need to sleep so I would take Xanax and Loritab just to be able to fall asleep. Sometimes I had cocaine withdrawal which I didn't even think was physically possible. However, my eyes would get very strained and watery and I would be wide awake for hours after I had done my last line. I would lay in bed while watching the hours pass. I would venture out into the living room where inevitably there would be lines of coke being done and the party continued. I would do a small bump from whoever was out there, and that would be enough for me to go to sleep. Eventually this sort of mass consumption of cocaine led to a hole opening up in my nose. For several years when I would breath through my nose, I could hear a sort of whistling sound out of the right side of my nose.

Max did a lot of cocaine and would stay up for days on end with his paranoia getting the best of him. He would be in the car which was running in the backyard with his guns pointed up at the pine trees. He was convinced feds were hanging out in the pine trees. His paranoia would eventually rub off on me. I would have my night vision monocle out back rolling around in the grass of the back yard. I was convinced the cops were constantly out to get me and It didn't help that my next door neighbor was a sheriff's deputy.

One morning in this seemingly never-ending cycle of drug-fueled craziness stood out. I woke up to go to work and a bunch of people didn't go to sleep the night before. Max was in the kitchen with Burt held up by his throat with a gun pressed against his head. Max was convinced Burt stole $10,000 in a suitcase that would be used for his re-up money in Miami. I was standing there trying my best to convince Max that this isn't worth it and that Burt was part of our crew. He just simply wouldn't do him dirty like that. My close friend Lucas woke up and came out of his room that he rented. He took one look at all the craziness in the kitchen and quickly exclaims, "I'm going to work." That was all he had to say about that because he wanted absolutely no part of whatever was about to go down.

Janice, Max's girlfriend, came into the house and told Max, without knowing what craziness was transpiring in the kitchen, "Hey honey, you left your suitcase in the driveway!" Things then began to settle down and Max let Burt go. It was back to business as usual after a quick apology. I understand to a degree how close it came to Max killing Burt because that world is full of betrayal and lies. Living with that mindset while having a large amount of drugs as well can never lead to anything good.

One day when I was asleep Burt was cleaning the shotgun in a room that housed a kilo of Max's cocaine in it. The shotgun went off on accident breaking a hole through the top of the roof and into the soffit outside. This sent Ralph into a frenzy! He took off running down the street at two in the morning with no shoes on. He said later, in his high-pitched voice, that he had seen alligators. He was hiding out in ditches and somehow ended up getting bloody. Later, he wound up at Cracker Barrel several miles away a little after five in the morning. He said he was waiting for Cracker Barrel to open. However, he scared the workers there enough that they called the cops on him and was picked up for trespassing. Fortunately for the rest of the house, no further incident came from the shotgun blast. We were pretty concerned though!

Cocaine was making everyone paranoid but money was coming in and the party couldn't stop! One day I came home from a party to find that someone stole my safe. They had broke in through a back window, and just picked up the entire safe. I had about $7,000 of cash and drugs inside. It was a little setback but I could bounce back. It definitely made me aware that I was a target and people were not truly my friends. It made me not trust people on an even deeper level, and always be apprehensive. People on the inside had provided that information.

I always believed in diversifying when possible and I had the chance to invest in a grow house. A grow house is a piece of property used to grow marijuana primarily. I only sponsored them one time but the sights and smells of going into that house with marijuana growing everywhere is unforgettable. I always loved a good smoke and had quite a collection of glass bongs and pipes. It helped that one of the guys I sold to worked at a wholesale bong and pipe distributor. I would sell him a few pounds and a couple hundred pills a week. However, cocaine was the primary cash cow at this point.

On New Year's Eve in 2005, I walked up to the party with a backpack full of bagged up eight balls of coke, quarters, ounces, plenty of weed, ecstasy pills, and Loritabs, people knew what time it was. I set up in a bedroom and everyone would be banging on the door to get in. People were so ready to party I could barely take a break myself! I sold out of everything and made over $2,000 profit in six hours all while partying my ass off. That was not a bad hustle for a 20 year old.

To celebrate, I took about $5,000 I had been holding on to and decided I was going to blow it all at the mall. I took my crew with me to mall of millennia in Orlando and I told them we were going to blow it all before we left. We had a great meal at a high end restaurant where I felt everyone was staring at us. I bought a $300 paperweight, some Timberlands, a new night vision set and a bunch of other stuff that I had no need for. But I blew all this money in hopes to fill a void. The void of my mother who was gone. That, in my eyes, I was now successful at something. That success I thought would make me happy.

At the end of the trip in Orlando I got the call that Max needed me to drive him down to Miami to re-up on a kilo. I normally sleep after doing coke however we also popped Ecstasy so we were unable to sleep. The whole crew had been up for at least 36 hours at this point. I didn't really feel like taking the trip. But I was almost out of my own personal stash of coke and Max was our re-up guy. I told him the crew would be on the way shortly to get him. I eventually made it to his house around eight that night where I then picked up Max and headed straight toward Miami using the Florida Turnpike. We showed up to our spot near Okeechobee Road around eleven later that night.

We were fairly cautious about things; we changed out our cell phones monthly, had other names we used (Max was Max Payne, I was James Cannon. Ralph was Bob Dole.) We had removed our cell phone batteries and sim cards, so as to avoid any form of tracking from them. Ralph, Burt, and Burt's girl were in the back seat; Max and I in the front. When we made it down to Miami, at about 11, we show up at the spot, down near Okeechobee Road.

Max went in to the spot with his backpack and stayed inside for a few minutes. One car came by and picked up the backpack while we were just sitting and watching because we didn't know what was going on. Then a white Mercedes came up having no lights on and without a license plate. Two gangster looking Cubans thin and tatted with a bag came out and they went in the house. If some gangsters are going to ride around in a brand new Mercedes without a license plate at eleven at night, you know they are ready for whatever comes their way. They came out with the re-up bag and then Max returns to the car after a few more minutes. The process seemed to take hours, but it may have been thirty minutes from start to finish. I was tired and happy to be on our way after watching all of this take place.

Before we could leave, of course we had to try out the yay-o, the Spanish slang term for cocaine. We stopped at a gas station on Okeechobee Road where we hit up a good line each. It was straight fish scale and right off the boat, as people in that world say. We were not tired anymore! We took the turnpike back home and of course we were totally paranoid. Between no sleep and a kilo of coke in the bag on the floor next to Max, we had every right to be paranoid.

Just because you are paranoid doesn't mean they're not watching you though. As we made our way back to Palm Bay, there was minimal traffic because it was around three in the morning. During our travels northbound on Interstate-95 we came across a brown Crown Victoria that was parked in the emergency vehicles only area between the north and south-bound lanes of 95. As I watched in my rearview mirror, the Crown Vic creeped into the northbound lane. We were going the speed limit and not doing anything obviously wrong, but the Crown Vic decided to pull behind us when we would approach an exit. Once we passed exits, while still driving on the interstate, the car would go ahead of us because there was no exits on this stretch of road. Once we got back towards an exit he would then creep back behind us and we then knew what game he was playing. When we got close to our exit we got off the interstate and the same car followed us and took an immediate right. There is no reason I can think of, other than following us, that a government vehicle would come from Port St. Lucie, travel to Palm Bay, several counties north, and then just turn down a road that is a quarter mile long and just has a cul-de-sac at the end. There was no doubt in my mind that we were followed.

As I crept through the back streets Ralph said many times in his highly nasal voice, "Mark I gotta piss". I said, "You piss in my car I'mma piss all over you!" That shut him up for a while. I was seeing cop after cop after cop on those back roads. We crept through the back streets certain we were about to get pulled over. Max had one hand on the bag and the other on the door. That readiness to jump out the car with the craziness in his eyes and voice told me just how dire and serious this situation was. We headed over to meet up with Janice in West Melbourne with our logic being that if we at least out of the city of Palm Bay's jurisdiction we could possibly be better off. Max got into Janice's car with the coke while the rest of us headed back to my place in Palm Bay. I knew it was just a matter of minutes before my house is getting raided due to being followed all this long. I had some drugs there so we did all the coke we could, smoked a blunt and flushed the rest to get rid of evidence. I flushed about 100 Loritabs and Xanax. I was not trying to get caught with all that. However, the cops never came that night but I did learn something important. Next time we head down south to re-up don't take the turnpike because they could easily monitor how long you were there, and stay in Miami longer than a few hours late at night. It would be the first of many trips down south, and one to learn from. Like Master P says, "The Feds Be Watching"

Around this time, the crew moved. They followed where I moved out near the "compound" which was several miles of nothing but streets with no street signs and sometimes hardly any street underneath all the overgrown weeds. There were potholes that could actually swallow cars if you weren't careful. Around this time I got tired of driving to my day job, so I quit for good after about 6 months. It wasn't like I needed the money, but the routine was good for me in some ways.

Max's paranoia grew more intense as time went on. His episodes became more frequent and his behavior more erratic. Someone I sold to named "Jewboy" lived out there about a mile away from us and Max decided to go on this run with me. Max started waving his gun out of the car and pointing it at trees, thinking they were federal agents. There wasn't much civilization out there so I didn't mind TOO much…. I could deal with a lot from him. But I would always tell him there are not any feds out there and he would put it away. Some times he would listen and other times he would not. It all just depended on how he was feeling and whether I was his homeboy that day or not.

Max would stay up days on coke and he would have us drive him around the neighborhood that contained only a dozen houses for a mile around. Max would walk up to trees with guns drawn looking for the feds. He had bloody knuckles several times from him apparently knocking feds out. This shows the extent of his paranoia and hallucinations.

One morning after doing a bunch of coke Max ran out to the compound barefoot. Three hours later we found him several miles away at his girlfriend's-mom's-house. His clothes were torn up and his feet and fists were bloody. We figured he had been running through the woods in his crazy stupor. Through all this, he still had the sense to keep the drugs flowing to the crew.

On one trip to Jewboys so I could make a deal, Max went inside and handed random girls four-thousand dollars in cash before running back into the street. I was more interested in watching his cash than whatever craziness he was getting into, but when he came back, his fists were all bloody… he had been punching palm trees down the street. I managed to keep track of his money as best as I could while doing our deal. One time Max's paranoia rubbed off on Jewboy, and Jewboy flushed a $900 ounce of cocaine down the toilet in the belief that the cops were en route. He then spent the next few hours breaking apart his toilet, smashing it into a hundred pieces with a hammer in the hopes of retrieving it. Cocaine is water soluble, so there was little chance for him since it wasn't wrapped up perfectly.

Max continued down this road of trouble and cocaine where searching for feds became a daily undertaking. After having no sleep for five days, I gave him a few Xanax and Somas to calm him down in hopes that he could get some sleep. A few hours later, with Janice driving him back to his house Max decided he saw a fed, which was a palm tree. He punched Janice, who was driving, in the face then steered the car into the palm tree to hit the fed. Then he tried to give people over ten-thousand dollars for a ride away from there. When the cops arrived they found four ounces of coke, the Xanax and Somas I gave him, a fake ID, twelve-thousand dollars, a bullet proof vest and a few guns. One of the guns was a police issued gun that was tied to a home invasion.

Obviously I was blown away by all of this but I decided that I was gonna bail my "boy" out (and also gain back my fire coke connect) for five-thousand dollars. Max skipped bail, avoided me for a few days and just screwed up. He tried to find any reason whatsoever to avoid me because he owed me money. Whatever! I was not trying to deal with all that drama. I was loyal to my business partner but loyalty is a falsehood in such a game. I was just glad I survived that period of life. The volatility became normal after a while, because it was simply my way of life at this point.

4. Post Payne

I was able to get a hook up with one of Max's important Miami connects, Pablo. When I could combine purchases of a quarter kilo or more Pablo came up from Miami. Pablo would travel in a limousine which was an uncommon site in the backroads of Palm Bay. Pablo also wanted to strengthen his out of town connects as he was having troubles in town at the time. A rival had recently attempted to blow him up while he was in his Jaguar, *Casino* style. Pablo rode in a limo because his logic was if the driver of the limo was pulled over they would have no probable cause to search the back half of the ride because it is a rented out space to a private individual who has appeared to not commit a crime or driving offense. I'm not so sure his logic was sound, but I wasn't going to question it as long as I got what I needed.

I had some good connects in town as well. J had the quality product at good prices. This all changed on July 1st 2005 when J got popped by the DEA where I watched it all play out on the local news. Here was a man who was balling by doing his thing with platinum everything. Just like that he is out of the game and gone. Life is all about choices. During this time, I did not care about those choices I was making because I had my own thing going on where I was going through an eighth a key every day. I had a crystal cup filled with an ounce of cocaine every day where I passed it around and partied with everyone I wanted to. I can't go anywhere without some junky from some party running up to me at a gas station. I remember this one guy at a 7-11 ran up like he was my best friend, named the party he was at, who he was with, and everything. Said I hooked him up with some fat lines. I couldn't remember him at all. Thats just how it was, making the insane my daily routine. It's not something to be proud of, and I wasn't proud of that fact back then. It's just simply how it was. This is one of the reasons I don't call Melbourne my home today.

I could always find something though. There is always a dedication to those in that world to make money, and where there is demand there is supply. Whether in town or down in Miami, I was going to make sure that I could supply the demand that came my way.

Things were crazy while living day to day and party to party. Line to line even. But those steady connections to a quality product kept getting busted or blown up. I sold what I could and used the rest myself. I kept going on this downward spiral of life. But it didn't matter to me, I thought I had all that I needed.

5. Katrina and Wilma

Hurricane Katrina came to the gulf states, and I wanted to get away from all the craziness of life partly because I was having a lot of drama with my ex girlfriend Devon. It is ironic that I wanted to go to a disaster zone from a storm to leave a disaster zone of my own creation. I moved out of her place and was living at my buddy's house where I did an occasional tree job just to make a little extra money from an honest day's work. Between that and hustling, money was decent. I liked the hard labor sometimes because it made me feel like I was doing something productive. But sweating out the night before would be no fun.

My good friend Carl and his brother Joe were going to leave to assist with hurricane cleanup in Mississippi. Joe had his own tree trimming business and was a certified arborist, and had all the equipment necessary. They asked if I wanted to go with them to help. I agreed because I was ready for an adventure. We loaded up with all the needed arborist equipment and supplies that we could possibly think of. They even created their own ramps so the bobcat could be loaded up in the dump trailer. Additionally, I loaded up with plenty of coke, weed, pills, and whatever else I could get my hands because I wanted to be prepared.

I knew I would see damage from the storm but I had no idea what I was in for. We went to D'iberville, Mississippi where there was damage EVERYWHERE. It looked like a bomb had exploded and damage was for blocks around. It was only a week after Katrina went through and there was still no power anywhere. Transformers were still blowing up on a regular basis, boats were everywhere even in trees and house or in the middle of stores or on cars…. Damage! Within a couple miles of the water there was nothing but debris and mostly unrecognizable structures and everything demolished beyond repair. I will never forget the most astonishing sight I saw while on that trip. As we got within two blocks of the shoreline where it looked as though there were just slabs of brand new construction. There was no debris anywhere because it had ALL been swept away by the storm surge and nothing remained. That sight truly showed me the power of a ferocious storm.

We proceed to stay in Mississippi for the next three months. There was plenty of work for tree removal and we were paid two-hundred dollars a day. It was good "legal" money since I barely knew how to run a chainsaw when I got there. I did not mind the break from life back in Melbourne because it was fun to see and experience something new and different to me even if it involved difficult manual work. There were hardly any stores that had food, and no housing whatsoever. For the first month, we slept in the dump trailer once we had removed all our daily debris from it. We had a generator, air mattresses, a George foreman grill and a portable AC unit. That was about it for accommodations.

We made our way to Hattiesburg, Mississippi and ended up renting out a burned down restaurant, which still had a roof and was much more comfortable than living in the dump trailer. We took trees out of farm houses for miles around and we were able to work seven days a week if we wanted too.

One night after a couple months we decided to get drunk at Ropers, the local "popular" bar in Hattiesburg, where our boss Joe decided to get plastered. He was always drinking but especially today. Without opening his mouth any additional amount, he proceeds to throw up, with this waterfall of liquor just cascading, almost gracefully if it hadn't been vomit, down his face and clothes and onto the floor. So we decide to throw Joe in his truck, which we had taken out that night. Carl and I keep drinking. We score an ounce of weed for thirty-five dollars and it was decent regs. I was kind of surprised by the cheap price, almost reminded me of being back home in Texas. Florida I never got prices like that.

Back then I wore glasses and I also drank quite a bit of alcohol. That evening at Roper's I lost part of my glasses frame making it very difficult for me to see anything. Somehow in my drunken escapades, I became convinced that Carl stole my piece of the glasses frame just to mess with me. Therefore, when we left Ropers we were fist fighting by the time we made it back to the place we were staying. I started swinging and Carl and I go back and forth for a good minute.

The truck all of our friends were in drove off and we figured they went back to the bar. Carl and I eventually made peace after throwing blows and we smoked a joint from the weed I had. A sheriff's deputy pulled up and Joe was just beat up, pistol whipped, and left on the side of the road way out in the middle of nowhere. They started asking us all sorts of questions and then asked if our boss was, a little funny or gay. The cops were insinuating that he brought the beating on himself. Instead of the cops trying to get the guys who did it they wanted to ask all sorts of garbage questions. The sheriffs saw my weed sitting on a book and decided they scored for the night by writing us tickets. When we could not produce an ID they instead confiscated our weed and give us a warning. They apparently didn't want to be bothered by the paperwork at that point. I wasn't exactly looking forward to having a court appearance in a Mississippi court several months away either. The Sheriff's deputies notified the owner the next morning. We were promptly kicked out of our wonderful burned down restaurant that we were staying at.

We ended up going to an old flower shop in Purvis, MS which turned into our new headquarters as there was still no lodging available anywhere around. We continued to take trees out of farm houses on a daily basis for the next few weeks. After the incident where Joe was beaten and his equipment was stolen things were not the same. One of the guys who helped secure the work went home which changed the dynamics of the entire operation.

When hurricane Wilma hits South Florida, one tree worker I am with decides to drive down there. I met my old buddy William from Texas in Naples where we camped out on the beach down by Marco Island. It was beautiful being down in South Florida and living on the beach while waking up to find sand dollars and beautiful shells amongst the tranquil waves. William was happy because he was able to go fishing before we cleaned up the tree debris. We only had a chainsaw in the trunk of the car to clear up storm damage. We were waiting until we were able to meet up with an arborist who gave us steady work again making around $200 a day.

We lived on the beach for a week until we found a house to sleep in. Over a few days, we cleared a giant Banyan tree from a property and the owner of the house invited us in to live. I decided made a beeline for my dirty doctor in Ft. Lauderdale where I picked up my monthly script of Loritabs. We decide to have a night of heavy drinking. We added in some Xanax with the Loritabs and got pretty drunk. William owned a late 90's Pontiac Grand Prix, which on the inside looked EX-ACTLY like my mom's old car. That always freaked me out a bit that he chose to get a car that resembled the car that was in the accident that we were all in when my mom passed. We left a bar and were heading down the road and William started speeding in a crazy fashion. He was barreling down the road doing at least seventy or eighty miles per hour around thirty mile turns. I was yelling at him to stop but he chose to ignore me and kept racing himself. Being back in similar surrounding that we were in before with the same car all while being drugged up… I snapped… I started punching him while he was driving because I wanted him to slow down. I now realize in hindsight that may not have been the safest thing to do. We pulled over to fight and after a few blows William got back into his car and took off down the road. I was so drunk that I just found a ditch in a commercial warehouse and fell asleep.

When I woke up in the morning I was a mess. Fortunately, I was able to sleep off the alcohol and drugs but I did not have my wallet, any of my stash, my cell phone or a way around other than my own two feet. I had no clue where I was. While we were working in Naples for a couple weeks at that time, we had gone partying around Cape Coral and I had no bearing at all where I was. I admit I felt pretty helpless and I was trying desperately to get ahold of William. Since our minds were thinking a little more clearly now we both realized how stupid we were being. I was calling his family back in Texas trying to get ahold of him because I was getting no where, his cell phone was off. I ended up sitting at a gas station by a pay phone for a few hours and finally we were able to find each other and settle everything. William was my best friend and we did not mean for all of this stuff to happen.

That day when I was walking around Cape Coral essentially as a homeless person without any money showed me how quickly life can change. Ultimately I made the choices that got me to that point and I took full responsibility for my actions. It was a realization of how life can change quickly, even if it was just a glimpse.

We met up with an Arborist who needed help with removing storm damage from trees around Naples. He was a good hard working guy, and we could appreciate his work ethic. We had steady work with him all around Southwest Florida. Eventually he won a contract to remove debris in Ft. Lauderdale and Miami.

When all three of us made the move from the west coast of Florida to the East coast, William and I got a place to stay in Miami. This time we upgraded from a burnt down restaurant to a nasty-partially-flooded hotel right by the Miami Airport. I get William into my dirty doctor, which as long as he had a pulse would not be a problem. Steady drugs, steady work, and steady partying. During this time I made one of the only good decisions I made during this chapter of my life and I had Lasik eye surgery. I decided it was probably smartest to see an expensive eye doctor in Miami. Vision is priceless! We had spent thanksgiving clearing out debris, but as Christmas approached the jobs were starting to slow down. It was time for a change, but also time to head home for the holidays.

I look back on the storm chasing portion of my life as a great adventure. Despite all the hardships I feel that I grew as a person. I learned how to become a capable tree groundsman and knew a thing or two about a hard day of work by the time it was all over.

6. Christmas Party

Christmas 2005 I decided to head back to Texas with William to visit my dad. We stopped in New Orleans to see all of the terrible destruction that occurred from Katrina a few moths prior. Every car was on blocks and the waterline was obvious on every building we saw. The only people we saw on the streets were in white biohazard suits. We did not stay long because we were a little freaked out by all the destruction. Also, we did not want to get a flat tire from all the storm debris still left on the road. Nothing but death and decay surrounded us and the waterline was a very clear and vivid reminder of the pain the city endured. I was taking pictures of everything like I had since arriving in Mississippi earlier that year. Unfortunately I lost most of them during the trip.

Back in Houston, I met up with some old friends from high school who were doing their hustle hard. I bought three-thousand Xanax and five-hundred Loritabs from a guy who offered to fly my shipments back on a plane if they were large enough. I had to keep that in mind for the future. The pills I bought wholesale at around thirty-five cents a piece. I could easily sell one-hundred packs for three-hundred and fifty dollar back in Florida. That same pill that cost me thirty five cents in Texas could retail for six dollars or more in Florida. In a club environment you could get ten dollars or more. I decided to stack my money off this little investment. Meanwhile, I was still partying and catching up with my old associates. One guy, who we are hanging out with a lot, really likes my white gold and mystic fire topaz ring. I wore a lot of jewelry, so I take it as a compliment.

I decided to take a greyhound bus back to Florida once Christmas was over. I had to get back before New Year's eve to supply the partiers. I figured there would be less of an issue while riding the bus than me driving myself. After our trips with Max Payne the year before to Miami I had learned to be a little more discreet in my travels.

Before I went back to Florida, our old friend who liked my jewelry said they had a friend looking for fifty Loritabs and one-hundred Xanax. Sure! I would be happy to make a little cash and not have to transport all this stuff back. We met up at an old farm house that we used to throw keg parties at in high school just outside of Fresno, TX. We were hanging out waiting on ole boy where there was a knock at the back door. The guy who set up the deal went to answer it when a man with a ski mask and gun pops out while screaming for us to get on the ground. While all of this was going on I decided to book it. I run out the back door. I was running as fast as I could while it was pitch black. There was nothing but fields around for miles and all I saw was darkness. Ole boy came out the house and fired in my direction. As soon as he started shooting I stopped. I didn't know if he could see me or what, but I really just couldn't handle trying my luck any further. I was not that far out into the field where I felt I could lose him. It was a knee jerk reaction because I did not want to die in that field that night.

Ole boy came behind me and pistol whipped me and he took me back inside the house. He took all my jewelry, of which I was wearing about $10,000 worth that night in rings, chains, charms, and watches. He took my drugs I planned to sell which was about fifty Loritabs and one-hundred Xanax. He took my wallet which contained about five hundred dollars cash then he ran off. Needless to say, I did not have a very merry Christmas that year. I was just glad I wasn't shot. Looking back I was able to see that I was set up by the guy who orchestrated the deal. He really wanted my mystic fire topaz ring and he created an opportunity to have it and much more. This guy was an old friend who I trusted as being one of our old crew turned on me in a split second. I was reminded again that there is no loyalty or trust in the drug game.

After Christmas I got on the greyhound bus where I figured it was best to store all of the Xanax and Loritabs on my person so I could have control of them and pop what I wanted on the long bus ride back. I bagged them up then put the bags in my jacket, my socks and anywhere else I could possibly stash them. As I hugged my dad goodbye at the bus station I could hear Xanax crunching. I don't remember much of that bus ride other than not feeling anxious at all about it. I arrived back in Melbourne and got my network cranking out these pills where I made back all the money that the guy stole from me. I took it as a cost of doing business because I was never into violence, I was just about the money.

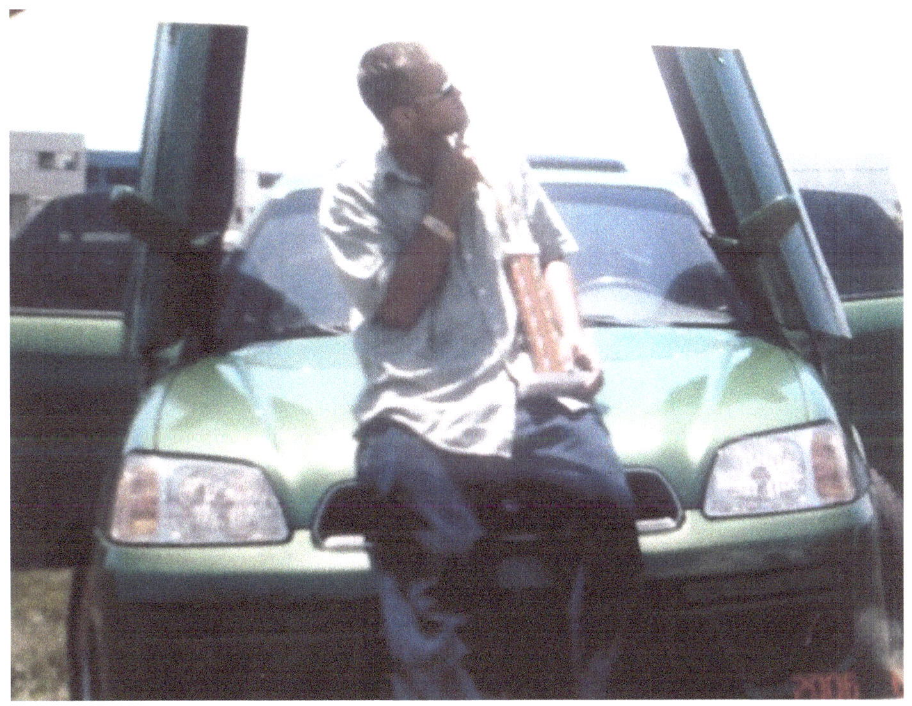

Mark with, "The Spaceship" after winning his first car show, 2006.

April 10, 2006, I decided it would be a good idea to get the biggest bottle of vodka possible and have massive martinis that were the almost the size of fish bowls. I was supposed to go trade an eight ball of coke for thirty hits of acid which never actually happened. Instead I decided to go to Burger King, buy a meal around 6pm, then drive down Interstate-95 heading south for no reason. Looking back, the only reason I may have been able to justify heading south was to re-up on cocaine, but I still had a good supply. I was going down the highway at one-hundred and ten miles per hour with all my LED lights on. I had a lot of lights on this particular car, which was called "The spaceship."

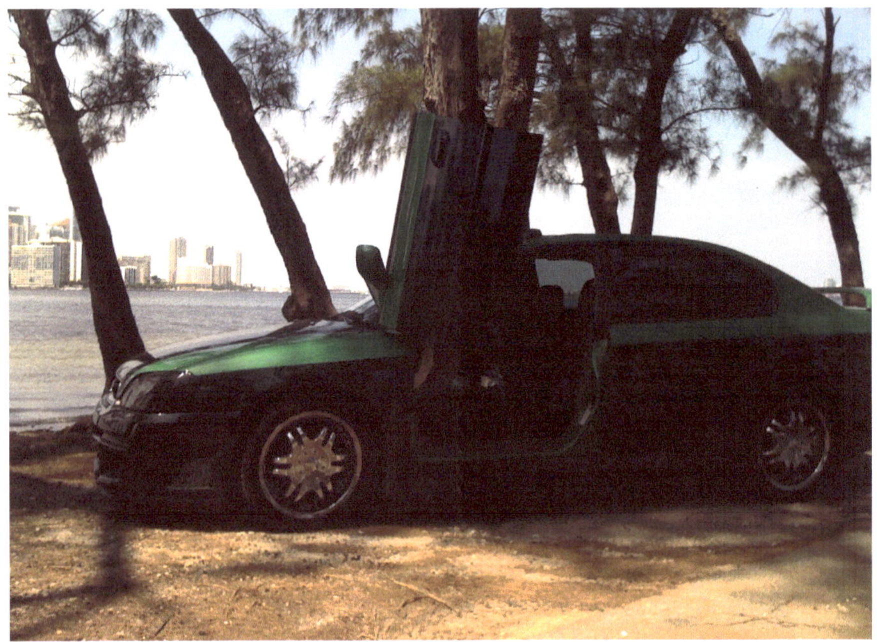

"The Spaceship" on a trip to Miami near Key Biscayne.

The next thing I remembered was being in the back seat of the cop car pulling into the Indian River County Jail. While in booking for my DUI charge the cops asked me to empty my pockets where the eight ball was stored. They ask me what that was and I replied, "Its Cocaine!" which landed me my first drug charge. The next morning I wake up….I'm still in a daze, trying to figure out why in the world I'm in Indian River County.

I always felt a bit low for that DUI. The person who was driving in the accident that killed my mom was sober. I often held it against them that they were speeding but what I did was far worse as I was extremely intoxicated. I was very lucky that I did not end up killing myself or someone else on that night or many of the other nights like that one.

I made bail and I decide that this lifestyle was not worth it anymore. I did not want to start accumulating drug charges and this charge would be a one off or a mistake. Once you become a felon your life is screwed. I had a pound of weed at my house and I decided to sell as much of it as I could and the rest I would cook into brownies. Each brownie ended up having over twelve grams of weed which is extremely potent! Additionally, I had three ounces of coke sitting at my house where I sold a bunch of leaving out about an ounce. Between that and a bunch of acid we have, we do up the coke, smoke the weed, eat the weed, drop the acid, and have a banging time. I would go out of that life with a bang before starting drug court and changing my life, or so I thought. I knew what I was doing, and I had control over my actions. If I just put my mind to it and applied myself, I could break the addictions. I could just be a normal person and go about my life. Maybe even sell a little on the side after drug court for some easy money, just not be wrapped up in all the rest of the drama. I could do that, right?

7. Life in Control

I started drug court because I had to get the cocaine charges dropped. I went through all the motions. I did legitimately want to quit on some level and I thought I was done with all the foolishness. I was twenty-two and I was ready to start over. I got hired with my mom's old company, Fiserv Lending Solutions. They specialized in mortgage processing and I worked in their shipping and receiving department. I decided to get a place with an old client of mine, a punk rocker who sells coke called Paul, near my new job. I could tolerate a lot of the foolishness that he was still a part of because I thought that I was stronger than that now. He was still selling about an ounce of coke a day combined with all sorts of other drugs including Roxycodone, also known as Roxies, which is the same thing as Oxycodone. These were just starting to get popular in our drug circles.

A year and a half went by and I remained sober. I didn't have much of a choice if I wanted to graduate. The drug court colors were randomly called for drug tests three times a week. One time when I couldn't find a ride, I pedaled my bicycle from Palm Bay to Rockledge so I could take a drug test at their facility in time. That is a twenty-five mile one way trip along parts of US1 that didn't have a comfortable shoulder to safely ride a bike on, but I was determined to make it. I graduated drug court, my felony cocaine charge was dropped and my year long driver's license suspension was removed. I was in control of my life for the first time in a while. I thought I was on top of this new sober world.

Paul had this girlfriend Lacey at the time who liked to get strung out on Roxies. Lacey decided to blow her brains out in the back of her SUV and Paul understandably lost his mind. He was huffing freon, sleeping at her grave, not coming home for long periods of time and not paying rent. He was already a loose cannon before Lacey's death but afterwards he was completely undependable. He was even disregarding selling drugs, so I knew for sure he is not going to be able to pay the rent. His customers kept coming by the house, asking me where he was, and I had no information to tell them. He would disappear for days or weeks at a time.

I convinced Paul that he needed help. But not the help that most would think. Paul gave me his stash to sell and I kept his clients happy. I paid him his money but I kept a little for myself. At that point we were basically in survival mode to make sure we had a roof over our head and could pay basic bills. He was basically getting a free place to live until he got back on his feet. Even through all this stress I was still not getting high.

I was in control. I thought I could get back into the game on my terms. I had proved to myself that I was not an addict and that my love of money could trump all the drugs. Paul told me how much money I could make from getting doctors to write prescriptions for Roxycodone from his dirty doctor, Dr. Jaiden. I found an old MRI I could use from my accident to make it seem legit. I had an established past of going to doctors for pain meds thanks to my dirty doctor down in Ft. Lauderdale from a few years before. All of a sudden I could go to one doctor's visit and make an extra five-hundred dollars a month with little extra effort. Eventually I was able to push Dr. Jaiden, and other doctors like him, to write me a script for two-hundred and twenty-four 30 mg Roxycodone, one-hundred and twelve 15 mg Roxycodone, and ninety 2mg Xanax at one time. I could make over three-thousand dollars profit which was more money than I made the ENTIRE month of working my legit job. Who doesn't want to double their paycheck each month?

I was not using any drugs because this was strictly a money thing. I had a goal of buying my own house and I had to keep the money coming in. I bought a house a few blocks down from my place with Paul in Eau Gallie and I put a twenty percent down payment. I started dumping a bunch of money into the improvements the house needed. I had to redo the landscaping, get a new air conditioning unit, put a safe in the wall as well as add cameras for security.

I felt things were going well because I could take care of all the financial issues I had and I felt in control. But after a few months of going to the doctor, they start requiring drug tests to verify you are taking your meds, but also not abusing any other drugs. This was done to verify the patient was actually taking the medication while not abusing other drugs. Therefore, I started taking my prescribed Loritabs only a few days before the doctor's visit so it would show up on my drug test. Around the same time I started getting a huge tattoo on my back. Ironically, the tattoo is a phoenix rising from the ashes symbolizing overcoming my former life.

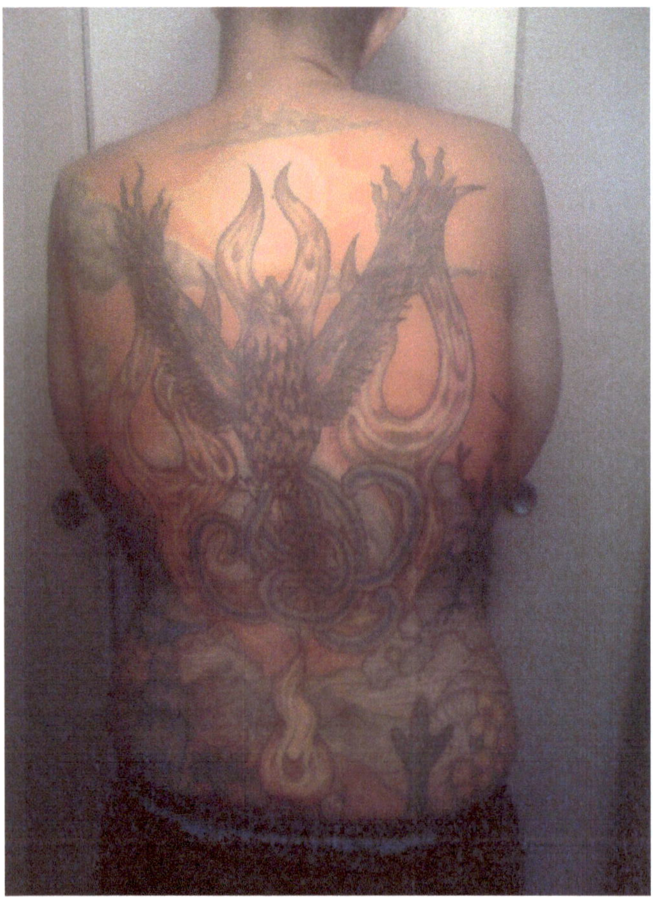

For the first time in a couple of years I ended up taking a 10 mg Loritab. I could feel the effects at night and most of the next day at work. I went to get my tattoo worked on every two weeks and all together I had over twenty tattoo sessions totaling sixty-six hours of work. Throughout that time I found out more and more that I did enjoy taking Loritabs. Especially the day after getting my tattoo worked on and I had to work it was a nice excuse to make the day chill.

By the time I finished my tattoo a year and a half after I started working on it, I went from taking one 10 mg Loritab to six 30 mg Oxycodones. That eighteen times more opiates than what I was originally taking my tolerance continued to grow from that point.

I kept going to the doctor where I graduated from Percocet and Loritabs to Roxycodone. This was a big break for me financially because this was early 2007 and I noticed an increase of people asking for "blues" or "roxies." Those were 30 mg Oxycodone pills which are often times blue in color. I sold out of my pills but of course my greed got the best of me. I got to the point where I was middle manning about fifty pills a night. Middle-manning is when you get a product from another dealer and sell it at a higher rate to make a profit. I started picking up pills for others, one-hundred or two-hundred at a time and selling them to other people quickly. The more I was around it the more I wanted to enjoy it for myself. One day I took a whole Oxycodone 30mg where I got really noxious and threw up rather quickly. But Maaaaan I was stoned out of my mind and it was memorable because I nodded out feeling really ly good. It was as though I was detached from my body, and I was perfectly ok with that feeling.

This is sort of the "honeymoon phase" that Oxycodone users experience where you can take a few pills and be blitzed all night. If I wanted to get really high I would just take another one. This reckless use of pills had not caught up with the rest of my life yet.

My use of pills started to spill into my work place more frequently and eventually I would pop them every single day. I would sell them at work, in the parking lot, and to coworkers. I took my prescribed drugs often and one day I took a valium which stayed in my system for a few weeks. Valium shows up different chemically than what I was prescribed so I got in trouble at work for that HR popped a drug test on me. After I failed the test, they made me go to a drug rehab class to keep my job. One day after class I took a dude back to his home and sold him three blues. To my surprise, I watched him shoot the pills up. This was strange to me because I just snorted my pills like most of the people I hung out with. That was the irony of pills because I was legally prescribed opiates and there was nothing they could really do about it. My sickening addiction would continue to go unchecked by anyone.

The demand for Oxycodone pills by my clients started to soon exceed the supply from my doctor. I started middle manning from other dealers to make a little profit far more than just my supply of pills from the doctor could manage. Just an easy $250 a night after work, and then by that time I could make about $2,000 from my monthly doctor visit.

I started to care less and less about my job and it started to show in my work. I was nodding off frequently and doing the bare minimum to get by. One night after making my daily run to a dealer's house I got pulled over by the newly formed Melbourne Street Crimes Unit. As soon as they said what unit they were with, I knew what time it was. They hadn't just randomly pulled me over for loud music or speeding. I had fifty 30mg Oxycodone pills and a couple dozen Percocets stored in a WD-40 canister with a fake bottom. Of course the officers found my stash and charged me with trafficking Oxycodone on November 10, 2008. My lawyer told me the charge carried a 30 year minimum prison sentence and encouraged me to co-operate in whatever way possible.

By this time I was past the honeymoon stage of my addiction and well into dependence on these painkillers to function on a daily basis. I was an addict and I could not think about a day without getting high. I went down a very dark journey and betrayed people I considered friends and business associates where I set them up to take the fall. It is not something I am proud of but I managed to escape a thirty year jail sentence. As they say, "it is what it is".

I was already on probation at work for the drug test I failed previously, therefore I ended up losing my job. I was booked for the arrest and missed work because of it, so there was no way I could hide it. In 24 hours, I had lost my job and faced with the problems and stresses of betraying people and looking at thirty years in prison. The arrest came to hit twice as hard and I sort of had a mental break down. I found myself sitting in my laundry room on a bucket, with a shotgun pointed to my head. I got extremely close to pulling the trigger a few times but ultimately decided not to. I was desperate and lost where I had no other escape except getting high as possible. I had the network and I could still sell full time. Thankfully, I had some money saved up so I could make ends meet.

Not only did my addiction grow but it spiraled out of control during this time. I managed to get into the "doctor shopping" business. Me personally, I only went to one doctor a month. I wanted to ensure I did not get red flagged by the DEA so I found a solution by sponsoring people and they would go to the doctor for me.

Sponsorship can work several different ways. If someone said, "I wanna go to the doctor and get pills." I could send them to get a fake MRI done by a dirty MRI clinic down south. It was actually in the parking lot of a Goldfinger's Strip Club in West Palm Beach, Florida. I would pay two-hundred dollars for a person to get a dirty MRI and then send them to a dirty doctor which cost about another two-hundred dollars on my end. Then, I had to fill their prescription by sending them to one of the pharmacies in my network of pharmacies I used, but also make sure they were able to fill it. My only goal was to get their pills. If a person came away with three-thousand dollars worth of pills I was getting $2,500 worth of the profit.

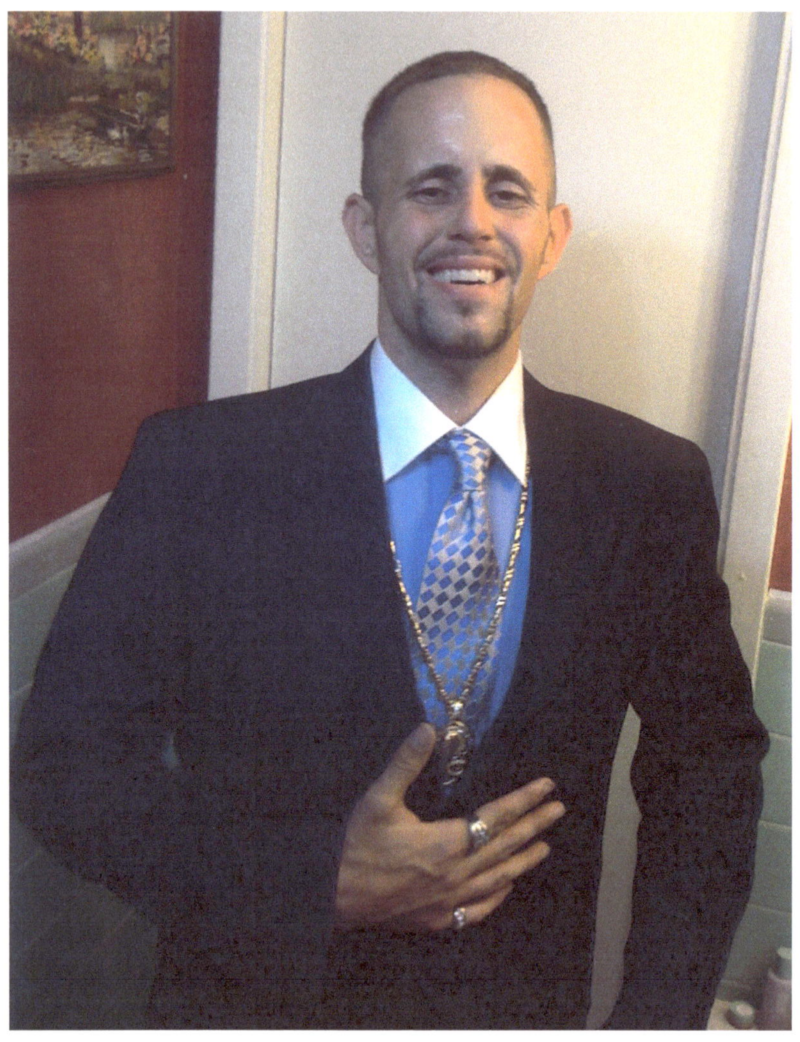

Mark, 2011

If a person was more experienced in the game by having their own doctors and transportation but only needed the cash, I would front the cash. As long as I made a profit I was happy. I would generally buy the pills at five dollars a piece resell one-hundred pills for ten dollars a piece.

This business just exploded by people who were wanting to get sponsored. I would have four or five trips a week to doctors often times down in Miami and Fort Lauderdale. Sometimes I would have multiple trips heading to different locations. I had eight people going to the doctor with me in one day. The math of the equation is simple; eight people who would each make me, on the conservative side, seven-hundred and fifty dollars adds up to six-thousand dollars for a day's work. Of course you still have to sell the pills, but you get the idea.

There was a guy who would come in with very elaborately painted mustangs named Vito. He was an Italian guy with gold jewelry, alligator shoes and he would smoke in the doctor's office because he owned the place. There would be a line of fifty junkies waiting for their turn at that office. People would pay between one-hundred up to five-hundred dollars to earn "VIP" status to get in to this doctor quicker. Mind you this is on top of their regular two to three-hundred dollar cash visitation fee. Often times, like Disney World, that VIP line would be almost as long as the regular line. Sometimes you would sit there from the time the office opened until the time it closed in hopes of getting prescribed pills. This was a daily occurrence throughout hundreds of doctor's offices in South Florida. Vito owned six of these doctors offices. Sometimes it was not that bad with a two to three hour wait. People in those waiting rooms would either be nodding out from the effects of the opiates or dope sick and miserable desperate for more pills.

I would take some trips and just have fun. I would just go blow money at the malls down in South Florida. Additionally, I went down to the Florida Keys and hung out with Carl and my boy Matt for a few days. We snorkeled and kayaked through the Marathon Key's Mangroves while smoking big cigars. My dealers and addicts knew my routine. Sometimes people wanted one-hundred pills or more in their orders. The routine was everyone would hold their pills on the way back to Melbourne to ensure that they were legally transported.

Once we got back to Melbourne I would divide the pills up and sell them as fast as I could to get them gone. I would usually sell more than five-hundred pills within a couple of house of being back home. I would purchase the oxycodone for roughly 2 to 4 dollars a pill and they would sell in hundred packs for 10 to 12 dollars per pill. The demand was insane. People would call and be waiting to meet up with me, scheduling people for 5 to 10 minutes apart for hours after I got home. This wave I was riding was so far from my control, despite whatever I had thought was capable just a couple of years before.

8. A Hurricane named Dora

Unfortunately the dealers and addicts I dealt with grew to know my routine. I normally stored all my jewelry in a safe behind a piece of art on my wall. I didn't like to travel a large distance and go to pharmacies and doctors offices with that sort of jewelry on. When I got home I found that someone had broken into my safe and stolen ten-thousand dollars worth of jewelry along with some pills and money I stored in there. It was an inside job.

Around this time I started dating a girl named Dora. She was an addict, like myself, and caught up in the life. She liked the money I made and the easy access to pills. I had her help out with some of the job duties but she wasn't very trustworthy. Often times things would come up short, and I hated thieves so I never wanted to believe it was her.

Dora would help me handle all the people. There is a ton of logistics involved in setting up doctors appointments, routes and drivers on a regular basis especially when everyone is detoxing and not fully functioning. Fortunately, in that world, money and pills were a good incentive to get most people to do what you needed them to do. She would handle and distribute the money for doctor's visits and pharmacies when I would have to stay in Melbourne to handle other doctor runs in a different part of the state or have to handle larger sales.

Our pill addictions continued to grow. I got to the point where I would snort ten 30 mg Oxycodone at a time. Even at the wholesale rate of ten dollars a pill that adds up to one-hundred dollars a line. A single pill could sell for thirty dollars in the right market. I would do thirty pills in a normal day on top of all the other drugs I was consuming. I never thought much about it other than I wanted to be high. I think part of it was an ego thing like, "I could snort you all under the table" sort of thing.

For a while I would get so stoned out of my mind that I would start nodding off at functions. One time when we were at Beef O' Brady's and I ordered chicken wings. I was moving them up towards my mouth in an effort to eat them except I was so stoned that I was completely missing my face. I was actually holding the chicken wing off to the right side of my face and then trying to eat the chicken wing. Life went on that way for years and I don't remember a lot of it.

 Around this time my house got robbed while my roommate was home. He was tied up and pistol whipped because they were looking for my drugs. I was out a celebrating my birthday with my girlfriend and we had the drugs with us. My roommate ended up getting his jaw dislocated because of what the attackers did to him when they were actually trying to get to me. That same guy had gone to a dirty doctor, and a nurse had used his social security number and stole his identity. Somehow he ended up having a car purchased in his name. Dude just had really bad luck I suppose.

One day I came home and some of my pills were missing. This started to be a common occurrence. Even though I would give Dora plenty of pills to take during the day that was not enough and she began to steal them. I would get severely upset with her.

Another day when I got home I noticed my buddy Carl was overdosing. He was not responding to the repeated attempts Dora made to help him. She started banging pots above his face and screaming at him. This had been going on about 30 minutes when I arrived home. I poured cold water on him and eventually resorted to kicking him to get him awake. He was STILL not responding from our attempts to save him or wake him up. I eventually gave up and called the cops because I had no other option. I did not want to take that heat from the cops but I knew that this was not worth his life. The paramedics came, administered Narcan and took him to the hospital.

Things began to really change. Laws were tightened up, shortages of the drug were occurring, and some pharmacies were refusing to fill prescriptions. All these things were making it harder to keep the supply chain constantly in motion. Being dope sick became more of a common occurrence. Dora and I pawned a bunch of stuff, which is something I never ever did, and used all the money to buy one-hundred Oxycodone pills. Dora and I went back to the house, wrote suicide letters and then each took half the pills. I snorted twenty at once and then popped another thirty an hour later. With Xanax, Somas and who knows what else in my system I thought that would be enough to do me in. We ended up both nodding off and the next thing we knew we woke up in the morning with the worst headaches imaginable. We very much alive with the brains that we had left.

On July 30, 2009, I was driving back to my house from Palm Bay while stoned out of my mind. I got pulled over and I received another DWI with pills. Once again more legal problems that kept the law on me. I ended up getting it reduced to a reckless driving charge and with the help of my lawyer I never faced a lot of consequences. While I was out on bond about two years later I ended up getting another DUI and I finally lost my license. However, that did not slow me down much because I could still get anywhere I needed with other people driving me around at the price of trading them a few pills. I still had an operation that covered the south and central Florida pill mills.

When I got arrested that time for DUI, I was so intoxicated. I was leaving a woman's house with ten 80mg extended release Oxycontins. Once I got pulled over, I decided to eat them all, since I didn't have a prescription for that particular version of pill. I actually had a prescription for oxycodone, but that did little good in jail. The staff assigned me to the bubble, the section of the jail designed for suicidal or extremely dangerous people, for my own safety. The bubble was worse than the box which was their disciplinary section of the Brevard County Jail. In the bubble you are put in a pod that is no bigger than a small living room with four of your closest friends. It is a tough place to be when you truly have no idea whether it is night or day because no sunlight can get in. No one is happy to be there because you are only allowed to go out to walk around in a slightly larger box with one small window twice a week. One guy that came in shortly after me was there because he just murdered his neighbor with a fillet knife.

I was in the bubble to detox snd boy-oh-boy did I detox! I would sweat and stink, because all those toxins were coming out. I would have things coming out both ends for days on end. When you are forced to share a toilet just a few feet away from people's heads and beds it gets old real quick. There was nothing to do in there with no escape. There were no magazines, books, paper or pen or letters. There is little chance to make a phone call except every two or three days. When your opportunity comes to make a phone call, it may be in the middle of the night. You do not even want me to describe the yummy food which was not much more than mush.

When the mental health examiner spoke with me that first week she asked me who the president was but I was so out of it that I could not answer her. I mumbled something back but could not make a complete sentence then I was sent back to the bubble.

My detox continued. I was laying there in my little sheet cocoon on the concrete (you don't have any sort of beds in there) just minding my own business, acting like i was asleep because I didn't want to be bothered with anyone or anything. And then the guards came in, unlocked the cell, and grabbed me. They dragged me by my sheet into a van. I recall them driving and talking as they drove me away from the jail. They hated my ass and told me that everyone else did too. They were just going to get rid of me. They manhandled me out into the swamp, and there was a huge alligator. I remember the alligator eating me, latching onto my legs and working it's way up.

And then I woke up in my cell.

Those hallucinations were so vivid and intense that I saw it as though it was really happening. This sort of detox happened on more than one occasion. In one case Jesus and the Devil were battling for my soul. I saw Satan as a dark prince, and Jesus with a mansion filled with many rooms. In my hallucination it was my choice where I wanted to be and I choose to be with Jesus.

I spent two weeks in the bubble which is a fairly standard time frame for people in my situation. Those two weeks feel like months simply because time drags on. They moved me out to the work tents where I was able to get in contact with my lawyer. My lawyer loved me because I gave him so much money over the years. He knew I was good for it so he put up five-thousand dollars of his own money to bail me out. I thought I would be able to repay him within a few days of getting out because I knew I had about eight grand sitting in my bank account.

I headed home and immediately took some pills. I was not able to take anything in over two weeks and it felt good to be back in that high state. I went to the bank the next morning and I had fifteen-hundred dollars in the bank. I knew for a fact I had much more than that when I went in. I knew someone stole money from me, but who and how?

I filed a fraud report with the bank and police report. I found out someone had been using my debit card when I was in jail. I asked the police officer to allow Dora to get my wallet when I went in. She swore it had been sitting in my house and no one touched it. The fraudulent charges happened in Palm Bay, Melbourne, and West Melbourne so she drove me to those police departments because I had to fill out a separate fraud reports for each jurisdiction.

After investigating it was discovered that Dora figured out my PIN code and she along with another person took my money out of multiple ATMs. While I was hallucinating in the bubble and unable to reach anyone in the outside world, she was taking my money without a care in the world for me. She was out having the time of her life getting high on my dime while I rotted in jail. This was a new level of betrayal that I never experienced before. This took several months to come out, and by then Dora had moved out, which was probably a wise idea on her part.

Even after this wake up call my bank account was still running low. I had to take the little bit of money I had left and hustle in able to get my lawyer his money. I knew not to play with lawyers and their money. So I flipped as much as I could as quick as I could. I sponsored a few people for doctors visits and I was able to get my lawyer's money back to him in about a week. It was a still a shock to me that I experienced such deep betrayal from someone that I considered to be in my inner circle of friends.

Before Dora moved out, we were fighting about her stealing my pills and she grabbed my shotgun which was loaded with buckshot. She jumped up on the bed and pointed it right at me so I jumped up after her trying to wrestle it away. I threw the barrel of the shotgun into my Tempurpedic bed when I heard a loud BANG! We both froze in our tracks. We both looked down and made sure all of our body parts were still there. I was finally able to secure the gun from her. That was a wake up call and she had to be out of my life completely.

Dora and I were officially done. I put a ring on her finger at one point but our addictions got the best of us. It honestly never meant anything to me because I did not know the first thing about loving anyone other than myself.

I started getting more and more sick because pills became even more difficult to attain. Regulations on doctor shopping and using multiple pharmacies became more stringent making it more difficult to abuse the system. I would get so incredibly sick that I did not care about anything except how I was going to get the next pill. With such a high tolerance I had built up one pill could not help me feel better from being dope sick. I would need three or four pills to make me feel normal again. So to just feel normal, it would cost me a street value of $90. It was such a miserable existence that I tried committing suicide a few more times.

One day a customer, Howie, came over to the house to get some pills. He then started acting a fool because he was really drunk. He even got belligerent with one of my friends. Howie and my friend started fighting, and because Howie was drunk he didn't stand much of a chance against this big guy. But I couldn't have fighting in my house, so I grabbed the shotgun and put the barrel up against the back Howie's head while he was on the ground. By this point I had so little regard for my own life that I did not care if I took his. This was a low point for me as I never thought I could resort to that level. He calmed down and decided to leave once he felt the barrel of the shotgun against the back of his head.

Oxycodone is a terrible drug that takes the life from you. A customer named Matt would work on my car so stoned out on blues that he would fall asleep. I remember one time he was doing an oil change which I paid him a few blues for. He got up to take a piss. He put his junk in his hand, pissing off the side of my car port. I went a few streets down to make a sale right quick, and ended up talking with someone. 45 minutes passed. I get back to my house, and there is Matt, still in the same position, still trying to take that same piss. He just nodded off in the middle of doing the job.

I have a blur of about five years because of all the craziness and nodding off during that time. I would doze off while driving down the road, in the middle of birthday parties, on the phone and anywhere else for that matter. In my mind everyone was doing it so it was ok. And part of the problem when you are in that lifestyle is that you surround yourself with like-minded people, so it truly becomes your new normal.

There was a lot of sad and lonely times. I was alone with my drugs and money. One Thanksgiving I got stood up by my girl-friend and hanging out with her family so I just smoked crack all night instead. I just wanted to get high and escape because I wanted to ease the loneliness and pain.

9. A Glimpse of Hope

Then I got together with Jenny. It was more of the same, business as usual for me. The operations started to slow, due to a number of reasons. The statewide regulations had started to really make it difficult to get Oxycodone, and people were getting switched to Dilaudid and other pain meds. But there was not the same profit margin in it, and people had to shoot them just to feel something. I knew Heroin was coming because people were going to chase that high they had started with pills. I didn't want to get involved because, in my mind, it was a dirty drug. Not that what I was doing was any better in any way.

I just managed to scrape by for another year and a half, being a junky. I tried committing suicide once during this time, but it was half hearted. Just locking myself in a bathroom with a gun kind of thing. I was just so sick of that life, and by this point it was all I knew, all I could remember being. A drug fiend who used others to support himself. Everyone I knew was in that life, and it seemed there was no way to get out on my own. At this point, the drug game had more or less been my daily existence for thirteen years.

I could see that the life was catching up with a lot of my people I had known for years now. People like Rick, who I had gone to his kid's birthday parties, just got so strung out. The joy had been robbed from people's lives. We just lived to get by, and not feel sick day to day.

My car got stolen by an ex girlfriend. I wasn't driving it regularly since my license was suspended, and it wasn't at my house. It ended up in a junk yard. It had been sold with no title and been parted out. When I saw it, the Lamborghini door was hanging off the hinge. It was kind of a sign that my time in that life was over. I was miserable, and it showed. I fought constantly with Jenny and her family, and no one really wanted to be around me. My relationship with Jenny deteriorated. I was washed up. It seemed every day was merely chasing an existence I had had, and just trying to maintain. But nothing got better in any major way.

The only good thing that happened in my relationship with Jenny was that she convinced me to go to church. We went a few times and I eventually I felt convicted about my sin and wanted to ask Jesus to be my the Lord and savior of my life. I walked up at the end of one of the services and responded to the invitation. After praying and feeling convicted, I began my relationship with Jesus. This was such an experience of a weight being lifted off my shoulder because I was sick and tired of being sick and tired and felt completely hopeless. I was willing to try anything because my life was not working out on my own and I needed Jesus because I was out of control. I was still an addict and still deep in that old life. But God had a plan!

I spent a few more months on my own and I did little deals on the side. I was trying to finish up my probation while flying under the radar because I was almost done with it. I was doing community service hours at a local thrift store where they had all sorts of sweet deals that came in. Additionally, I could take my side hustle up the street to meet people on my break. I felt like I was starting to get my life back on track some even if I was still an addict.

In late September I generally started looking forward to the cold fronts that come that time of year. The summers in Florida are so hot and long that by late September I was over it. My favorite weather of the year is when the first cold front comes through usually in the middle of October. Just cool enough where I do not sweat when I would walk outside.

September 26, I talked to Jenny and we could actually be civil for once. She told me that she found some things of mine at her mom's house and she wanted to drop them off for me early the next day because she had to work. We agreed to meet at the thrift store the next morning. She also mentioned she had a new boyfriend because she liked rubbing that stuff in.

September 27, I woke up like every other day except that day I was out of blues. I had to get my hustle on for any sort of drug soon whether it was a Percocet, Oxycodone, or Dilaudid. I needed one by lunchtime or else was going to get violently sick. I was also out of cigarettes which pissed me off. I decided to go up to the thrift store early in hopes that I could meet up with Jenny. I figured I could bum a cigarette off of her. I was waiting for the store to open when this big white guy came up to me. He asked if I was Mark Krancer and I told him yes because I figured that Jenny asked her boyfriend to meet me.

The guy pulled out a Brevard County Sheriff's officer badge and informed me that I had a warrant out for my arrest. A blue Ford Focus with New York plates zoomed into the parking lot along with a mini van. At this point they haven't even told me what I am charged with. But I ask continually. Finally, as they are putting me in the van, they say it is for sale of Oxycodone. At this point, honestly, I am relieved. As strange as it may sounds I was actually relieved. I felt sick and tired of the life I was living for years but I felt trapped in it. This could be a clean break for me and I might actually be able to get clean. God knew that I was powerless to quit drugs and leave this lifestyle on my own and this was HIS way of breaking those chains in my life.

I wasn't going to get to experience that first cold front, or many others. But I was going to be able to do something much more valuable: invest time in getting clean, going "cold turkey".

10. Jail

Eventually the cops took me to a sheriff's substation in Palm Bay, where I am placed in a paddy wagon with none other than Jenny and her brother Hank. Turns out my friend Rick became a confidential informant back in February and bought a series of pills from all of us. I was named the ringleader and the authorities wanted to get me. This was already in the works for months before I began my journey with the Lord. Then and now, I am far from perfect.

Jenny and Hank, while they were no angels, never had any serious trouble with the law therefore they were let go with probation. I however was already on probation for my DUI. The first time I talked to my public defender on the phone he mentioned that the district attorney wanted to give me five to twenty years in prison. That is hard for anyone to wrap their head around, yet alone a young twenty something. I just let things play out, and see what better offers the court may come up with.

I was not able to sleep during this time because I was still detoxing from all the drugs in my system. It would be six months before I would feel normal again or as normal as one can feel in jail. My body was so weak from all the muscle relaxers and inactivity that I could barely do five pushups. I started watching my health for the first time in years and I began exercising. I walked loop after loop around the communal jail cell, did pushups and dips. It was slow going but I stayed at it and I lost about thirty-five pounds. It was pretty easy for me to lose weight in jail as there was nothing to do on a daily basis. If there is one thing you have in jail, it is definitely routine.

I kept delaying the legal side of thing as much as I could because that was what the jailhouse lawyers told me to do. By this time I could not go anywhere in the jail without knowing someone I sold to or was associated with in some way. That was not a good thing as you always have to watch your back in places like that.

My hustle behind bars was to have guys sneak in cans of tobacco dip where I would then trade for commissary. Every now and then I would chew some dip because it was easier than trying to get a cigarette.

I began going to Bible studies and part of it was to have a routine and do something other than just sit on my bunk. However, I was genuinely interested in learning more about the Lord and growing in my relationship with Him. I realized that everything I knew and all the people I interacted with had a thought pattern that was dangerous and kept fueling the fire of that addictive lifestyle. I choose to seek out people who also experienced a change of heart. I learned that I must always be careful of the company I keep!

Time went by and I was working around the jail in various positions. Mostly this involved cleaning restrooms or hallways around the jail. This was not too bad as it made time go by quicker than just sitting on my bunk. Soon enough the days turned into weeks which turned into months.

The district attorney gave my public defender another offer of ten years where I immediately declined again. Christmas went by and I saw glimmers of Christmas decorations from the back of a paddy wagon while heading to court. The district attorney gave a third offer in late January which was for me to serve a year and a half and my time that I had already been in would count. SOLD! As I was told by the seasoned jailbirds prison time is much easier than time spent in county jail. So going, "Up the road" would be easier for me. A year and a day is much better than a year because once you hit that year point you go to the fabulous Florida Department of Corrections Prison system.

Now that I had a definitive sentence I could see the light at the end of the tunnel and I had goals to achieve. I did not want to just waste away from my sentence but rather wanted to use it to my advantage. I was through with that life from then on and only wanted to think about the future. Being healthy and clean from drugs with an abundance of time really changed my outlook on life.

10. Prison

In case you have never been to prison let me tell you-it is not a place you really want to spend any time at. Early one morning I was bussed from Brevard County Jail to Central Florida Reception Center in Orlando. When I arrived I had what the Department of Correction's equivalent to a drill sergeant yelling in my face. I was processed, given white boxers and was told to stand in line with three-hundred of my, "Best buddies." Then I was stripped of all my personal belongings and my head was shaved. I had to stand in a straight line with my nose right up against the person's head in front of me. It is imperative that everyone kept their eyes straight at he guys head in front of them. My photo was taken and then I was forced to wait. The saying ,"Hurry up and wait" certainly applies to all aspects of prison life but especially to the first day. Everyone is given five minutes or sometimes less to eat every meal.

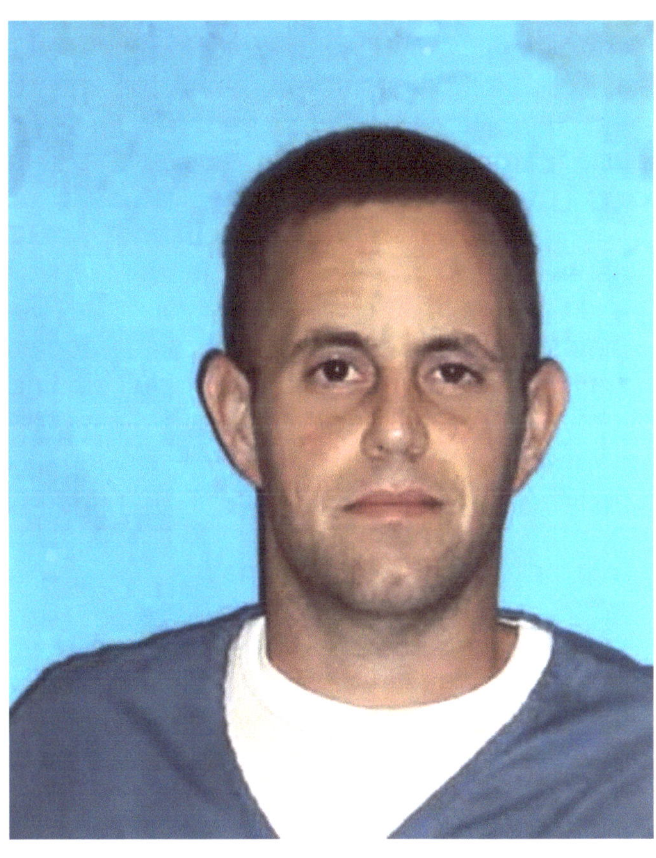

At count time, I would say "Krancer E27214 Sir"

It might not sound that bad until it is actually forced upon you. I usually eat fast most of the time so I learned to deal with it rather quickly but it was very difficult for some people. Sometimes that five minutes would turn into three minutes of actually being able to sit and eat which caused problems. Showers would sometimes have hot water but not always. This was the life in prison of never quite knowing what I was going to get.

I got assigned a cot then began the classification stage. My mental capacity was tested and a security rating was assigned to me based on current and prior charges. Fortunately I was classified as minimal security which does not really matter as I was able to go anywhere in the prison system. People are placed side-by-side next to people of all sorts including, "Lifers" who have nothing to lose. Drugs, rapes and shakedowns are all common occurrences in prison and gangs were all over the place. I could go to the yard twice a day usually which was nice for making the time pass by quicker than jail.

I got fully classified after a month and I was transferred to the panhandle where most of the "fresh meat" ends up. I went to a short timer's prison, where everyone has five years or less to their sentence, called Quincy Annex. People who are lifers could not go there, but some people could have spent thirty or more years being down and just have less than five years left. It was a place where people were looking forward to being done with their time and ready to get on with their life. Gang activity was still very evident as I saw people get busted up with locks in socks many times.

I got assigned to dorm B2 and I had just over a year left of my sentence by the time I arrived there. A year was just enough time to focus on what I really wanted out of life and figure out how to improve my future. I decided to write it down and I created lists for everything I could think of. I wrote down inspirational Bible verses, possible places I wanted to live, good workout routines, business ideas, and even bands I liked. I wrote down anything I read about that was interesting to me. It was ideas to channel my life and to make it how I wanted it in the future. I eventually made a large book that was stapled together with a cardboard front and back, named "The Quincy Papers" as I was at Quincy Annex in Quincy, Florida.

But before I got to most of "The Quincy Papers", there was dorm B2. In that dorm I had one friend, Stephen, who worked out like a crazy person. His workout would put to shame people that were half of his age. He looked like he was ready for a cover shoot with Muscle and Fitness because he was so physically fit. He brought that intensity and discipline to everything he did like his Bible studies, his preparations for being released and his personal routine. Steve helped me get into shape and really push myself through HIIT workouts (High Intensity Interval Training). I sprinted, did mountain climbers, burpees, crab walks and all sorts of other innovative workout routines while in prison.

Steve started encouraging me to go to chapel with him. I brushed him off sometimes because it started so early but eventually I attended with him more and more. The joy someone encounters in a prison chapel is impossible to replicate. Men can be free in there, knowing that they are in the presence of God despite their oppressed surroundings. Hearts are overflowing with joy like one can only experience while in prison. I have rarely encountered a choir or praise team in the free world that would sing filled with joy like people in a prison chapel.

Eventually I was allowed to go beyond the gate and I became part of the infamous Florida Chain Gang! Although no actual chains are used on a regular basis in that sort of work, the name still carries on. I got assigned to a road crew that went to the Florida Highway Patrol school kitchen near Tallahassee. We cleaned up and mowed the property. It was the best feeling in the world to be from behind bars and to be part of the "free world" even if it was just for work. Time passed much more quickly when out on work release because it gave me something to do and to look forward to. Simple things like peanut butter sandwiches that were microwaved were incredible! I did not have access to a microwave for a year at that point so that was a huge deal to me. I was able to sneak food away from the kitchen at times which turned out to be a nice form of payment.

One day, we are in the woods, the crew of 5 of us and our DOC guard. Our guard was a character. He was a skinny black, country guy and he did not care about much in regards to us. He would treat us like garbage because we were inmates and something less than him. One day he choked a guy out with a vacuum cleaner chord. Every now and then he would be cool with us but for the most part he always let us know that we were scum.

One day in April a big, pregnant diamondback rattlesnake came around our truck. We had shovels and a barrel with us so we threw a barrel on top of it. When we lift the barrel up, we beat the thing to death with shovels. The guard ended up giving the snake to someone on the property who fried it up. We got to see the eggs inside the snake before it was transferred to the cook.

Another time on a different road crew where we weed eat the Gadsden County ditches. This time two rattle snakes came out jumping all around us. I heard stories of people getting bit by rattle snakes while under DOC supervision. The process to get an inmate to the hospital is a long and arduous one which can put a life in serious jeopardy. Instead of taking an inmate directly to the hospital they would first be taken back to the prison. From there you are at the hands of the bureaucracy to get you to a hospital in a timely manner. When I saw those rattlesnakes I knew we both had to get the weed eaters and chop them up. Weed eaters are much easier to use than the shovels!

Other than rattle snakes and peanut butter sandwiches, life was pretty quiet. Pretty routine, other than the lock downs from time to time due to attempted escapes or contraband shake down. Even that stuff was pretty routine. As long as time continued to pass as quickly as it could, I didn't mind. And the road crews greatly helped that happen.

 I heard about work release from the time I was sentenced to prison. Work release is when an inmate works a legit job and can save some money for when they get out. A person on work release would get more freedoms and they were in the free world most of the day. That is what I wanted. I applied for it, and classification put the request through.

Steve got released and I was incredibly happy for him and his chance to start over. He sent letters updating me on how his new life in the free world was going. It was wonderful to hear about his success and new found freedom as we had sat around for hours talking and making plans prior to his release. I was on my own but I was settled in my daily routine and had a few people to talk to. I was certain to stay away from anyone who was trouble.

11. Jacksonville

As I sat in my Quincy dorm, I was not sure that my application for work release would ever go though. Late one evening I was informed that I would be transferred out the next morning. They approved my work release! I applied to work in three different places including Tampa, Melbourne, and Miami. After my initial transfer to Northwest reception center, I was informed where I was heading — Jacksonville! Wait…Jacksonville? I didn't sign up for this place, that isn't even Florida in my mind! But…the powers that be wanted me in Jacksonville, so off I go. Little did I know what the Lord had in store for me.

I was on the bluebird bus and for once not shackled up. Maybe because the classification department decided we were not threats because we were going to a minimum security place. I passed through Jacksonville once before when I left the state because of a hurricane in 2004. We arrived at a brand new facility which looked like the Ritz-Carlton compared to the places I was before. They had paint on the walls of their two-story building and plants on the perimeter! Me and my fellow prisoners were very excited about this new facility. Life will be sweet at Work Release!!

I get off the bluebird bus. We get processed, one at a time. There were people assisting us in plain clothes and the place had civilian feel in a sense. It is common to get sensory deprivation while behind bars because everyone is in uniform and everything is a material of DOC. This place in Jacksonville was completely different from the rest of the places I had been. We were the first group to arrive because the facility was brand new. The guards and staff looked brand new as well. We settled in and are called to a meeting where there is only twenty prisoners in a facility designed for two-hundred.

During this meeting the staff informed our group of several things including the rules, policies, and procedures. The biggest shock of all was that we were not in that facility for work release. WAIT?? WHAT?? We signed up for work release! We were trying to get jobs so we could start over once we were able to get and have a little savings or head start. Nope!

This new facility in Jacksonville was called Therapeutic Community. This was for drug offenders with less than a year left on their sentences. We will NOT be leaving the facility because we will NOT have jobs outside of these walls. We will be in intensive drug classes each day and must pass through certain levels until we "graduate" to be released from prison. We were told to address other inmates as mister and form an inmate led leadership council. I was voted as the secretary. We were all a little disappointed with the information we were just given and we needed to process it all. Who would have thought the Florida Department of Corrections would let a bunch of inmates down! To make matters worse, the other half of the facility was actual work release, so that just kind of rubbed it all in our faces that we weren't there.

But, shortly afterwards, I embrace this sudden revelation. I knew that I was an addict and that I needed help before going out into the real world again. I was determined to do whatever I needed to do to be prepared for the real world. These classes may be more beneficial to me than just sitting at a basic prison camp where nothing was done to benefit inmates transitioning back into society. Additionally there were huge benefits in this new camp including air conditioning and TV in the much nicer dorms. While the food was not exactly terrific, it is better than a regular prison's camp.

Each week a new group of inmates would come to the camp until the remaining dorms were filled which took about ten weeks. By then my group was considered to be the veterans and we were assigned to help out the newer inmates with orientation. I was a "big brother" and my "little brother" was a middle aged gentleman by the name of Gary. I looked out for him and many others during my time there. I tried to answer their questions and share in their misery to find out they were not there for work release. I became a GED teacher and helped tutor a few dozen inmates who ended up completing the course and they received their GED.

Some people smoked "toochi" or K2, the synthetic marijuana regularly. I watched multiple people turn green from the K2 no matter what their original skin tone was. I had no temptation to try this stuff, but it was passed around my dorm and the compound regularly. But they kept going back to these same things that would cause them to get really sick. An addict, just like me.

 Around this time I read a verse in the Bible that has stuck with me to this day: **"But now after you have known God, or rather are known by God, how is it that you turn again to the weak and beggarly elements, to which you desire again to be in bondage?" Galatians 4:9.** The Lord was saying to me that my old life was not worth it because I knew how God alone freed me from that life. We are surrounded by temptation and beggarly elements on a daily basis that weakens our ability to love the Lord and glorify Him through our testimony. This was also the first Bible verse I ever was able to memorize because of the power and direct relevance it had to my life, considering where I had come from and where I was now, known by God. I feel this was a real turning point for me spiritually, as I felt the presence of God in my life and the Word of God was alive.

I met another GED teacher named Jack. Jack was from Jacksonville and told me about this neighborhood called Riverside. He said if I decided to stay in Jacksonville, which I was considering at this point, I needed to move to Riverside. With my change of heart, I felt I needed the geographical change of somewhere new. He even drew me a map of the neighborhood to explain it to me. I had no way of googling information about this neighborhood or any other way to get info.

At this time I had about six months left of my sentence. I worked in the kitchen, I kept up my fitness routine and I always had a good book to read. I worked my duties as the secretary and continued to teach where I had access to some websites which helped me catch up with society. However there was no access to Facebook or other social media. While I was away, the whole hashtag thing became a big deal and I had no idea what was going on. When I would watch an ad on TV and they would say things like "hashtag Cadillac". huh? This is nothing though compared to some of the stories I have heard, such as people getting out and never even seeing automatic opening doors before! How do you help someone like that reintegrate back into society? It takes a lot of time and commitment for them to be successful, and they need more investment in their future than $50 and a bus ticket. When they are successful and don't land back in prison, that will save taxpayers far more money than whatever program is used to help them be successful.

There was a work release program on the other side of the facility however we had no chance of being placed over there. Once we were classified as TC there was no interaction with them. Occasionally while working in the kitchen we would serve them breakfast but there was little interaction. One morning while serving the work release group their breakfast a guy complained to me that his hard boiled egg was cold. They were supposed to be cold and always were. It just showed me how an attitude of gratitude can get you a long way in life. In prison there are so many people who are constantly incredibly negative. It can eat at you like a poison seeping into your skin. If you allow that attitude to keep a hold of you in the real world after being released you do not stand much of a chance. The downward spiral of negativity continues and the beast is being fed. Even with the great chicken revolt when half of the cafeteria was served raw chicken I was still able to be thankful for what we had.

A few months before being released, I had considered permanently living in Jacksonville. I knew that no matter what, I did not want to go back to those dark forces that had controlled my life, and that would have been much easier to get caught up in with people I knew from my past life in Melbourne. So Melbourne was off the table, no way I was going back there after I was released. It would be too easy to fall back into old patterns, old temptations.

I was encouraged to go to a Sunday morning service with Pastor Steve McCoy of Prisoners of Christ ministry. When I went I spoke with pastor Steve and told him about my situation. He encouraged me to apply for ministry housing where I would not have to pay for housing until I found a job once after being released. We had many visitors representing halfway houses, who basically stressed that we would need to not only find a job within two weeks, but also pay back those first two weeks rent. This can be incredibly difficult especially when trying to get back on your feet again and is not realistic. Prisoners of Christ was never about the money and they genuinely want to help men get back on their feet. They want to make the community a better place while sharing the love of Jesus Christ with men who were recently released. Pastor Steve invested in men by coming to visit regularly on Sunday mornings and throughout the week. He did all of this for the men on the inside still on top of running his ministry.

Pastor Steve taught many things and inspired me to have a deeper relationship with Jesus. This was encouraged by a daily devotion and praying out loud in groups. Something as simple as praying together can be difficult for people who have not previously been in church before and it was a truly powerful experience. It is a practical application of how to use the word of God. His love of The Word and of us prisoners showed me the level of compassion that God had given him and others like him.

While imprisoned at the Bridges, we also had service with chaplain Robert Brown. That man can set your soul on fire! The enthusiasm and high energy of his sermons, as well as his own personal testimony, was a great encouragement to the men. There were people who came because of free donuts and coffee of course, but in some way they were fed in more ways than just some food in their bellies. My first photography assignment was actually through chaplain Brown to cover a family day event that the prison was doing. "Chap" as we affectionally call him has continued to be a blessing in and out of the walls of the prison. I am thankful I see him on a regular basis to this day. It was the relationships built there that made transition back into society possible. With a lot of prayers along the way!

12. Here in the real world

One of the greatest blessings to happen through my time being incarcerated was the rebuilding of my relationship with my dad and stepmom. We had been distant for many years because of my drug use. Neither my mother or father had any issues with addiction, so I think they didn't understand how to help. I had reached out to my dad before when I was in trouble, but by the time I got arrested for my 2nd DUI it was falling on deaf ears. When I went away to prison I started to write him and continued to write him. Fortunately we were able to build a relationship again. He saw that the Lord was working in me and through me. They sent me a care package when I got to the Jacksonville Bridge, and we would talk on the phone. I think as time went on, my dad could see that something was changing in me. He was wary but optimistic. Family had not been a strong point in my life since my mother's death, but I was grateful to begin to mend those relationships. I praise God for the opportunity to open hearts and rebuild lives!

I became the first inmate from the TC side to graduate and be released from The Jacksonville Bridge. Not because I was special or anything, I just happened to have the shortest sentence out of everyone there. When you leave the Florida Department of Corrections, you are given $50 and a bus ticket wherever you want to go. That isn't much to start your life over on, but people make it work.

My dad and stepmom drove from Houston to pick me up from prison. That moment when they picked me up, I gave them great big hugs. None of us were sure what my future was going to look like, but I knew one thing, for the first time in my life I truly had hope. Hope restored by the power of Jesus in my life. Not only was I thrilled to be out, but I was excited to take this preparation I had been doing with my ideas and actually apply them to my life. All of this time was spent with that Galatians 4:9 verse strong in my head, about turning back to beggarly elements.

I had the simple pleasure of going into a gas station and buying what I wanted… that was amazing. I bought some peanuts
and a lemonade, and it felt so good to have that freedom. I
didn't have much commissary in prison, so I hadn't really had
a chance to buy anything while inside. But just the simple
freedoms of walking in a gas station and looking around is
mind blowing when you're released!

My dad blessed me with one-hundred dollars to help get
back on my feet which is twice as much as you get when you
leave prison. I purchased a cell phone to be able to communi-
cate regularly. I had everything set up so I could transition into
my new housing at the Jericho house, a home in Prisoners of
Christ's ministry housing located near Liberty street. I was so
excited to see whatever Jacksonville could offer. I had a few
hours with my dad and stepmom before I had to check in at
the POC house on 9th street in Springfield.

We went to the Landing that I saw on TV a few times. We had
no idea really what to do in Jacksonville, but it seemed like the

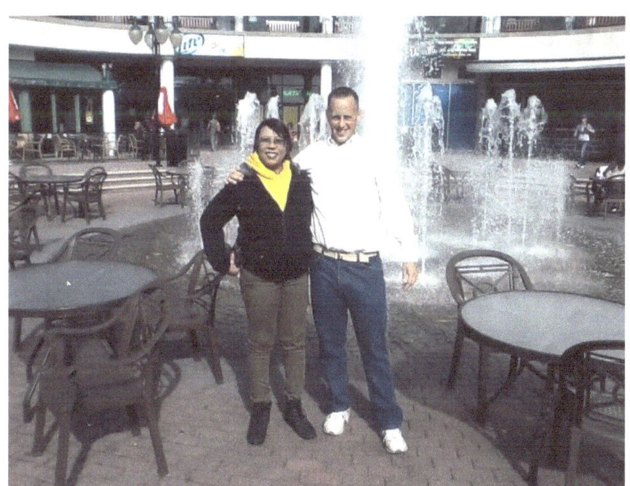

Mark and stepmom Diana, on January
5th, 2014. The day he was released
from prison.

place to go. I wanted to go see this Riverside neighborhood that Jack mentioned. We drove around the streets of Riverside and eventually turned the corner where I saw this beautiful statue in a park. It was the "Life" statue in Memorial Park. I saw the symmetry of the park and noticed how peaceful it was. It was only in passing that I saw the park but it's beauty made a lasting imprint in my mind. I never saw a park quite like this before and it was particularly inspiring considering the environments I was in for the past several years. Melbourne did not have parks that displayed the victorian era attention to detail as Memorial Park did. Riverside left an impression on me that remained. While passing Memorial Park I got a text on my new phone from someone asking how I felt being on the outside. I told them it felt pretty incredible.

I went over to the Jericho house and unpacked my blue prison bag filled with all my earthly possessions. I had a roommate, Johnny, who was also just been released and was as excited to be out as I was. In my new housing arrangement we had accountability partners we met with and talked to about our struggles and accomplishments. Chaplain Brown blessed me with a late seventies or early eighties Schwinn bicycle that was somehow still in perfect condition. I rode that bike EVERYWHERE to explore my new found freedom in the beautiful winter weather. The colder the temperature the better for me as I get really tired of sweating from being hot-natured.

I had a cheap phone and once I discovered the Jacksonville Riverwalk I took photos of pretty much everything to record the beauty of the world I was deprived of for so long. I was finally coming to realize that long before my actual prison sentence I was in a prison of my own making. In my self made prison I closed my mind to the beauty of the world around me and did not appreciate it until I was released. There is peace for me, there along the river with downtown as a backdrop.

Durning this time we went to Bible studies and church services, volunteered at the ministry and took classes to work on our resumes. I even became a certified volunteer tax preparer with United Way. It was a time of great personal growth, and the enjoyment of giving back while being spiritually fed was great nourishment to my soul.

 When a person is released from prison they get handed fifty dollars to help you start a new life. Upon your arrival at POC it is required to pay thirty-two dollars to pay for your Florida ID which is an essential to get your life back on track the right way. You cannot do much to re-establish yourself without identification. That means that a person has eighteen dollars remaining for everything else until you get a job. Thankfully with Prisoners of Christ the housing, food and toiletry expenses are taken care of. I vividly recall having to think about where I was going to get money to pay for nail clippers. It was just a simple item but at that moment the clippers were considered to be a luxury in my life.

Fitness had become a huge part of my routine in prison, and an essential part to my life. I considered it to be important to keep up after being released. I tried to explain my situation to some gyms and I offered to help clean up in terms of payment but I was scowled at, rejected and asked to leave. All I wanted to do was workout and no one wanted to give me that opportunity. I managed to get a membership at the downtown YMCA through their financial assistance program. Dee from the ministry paid my fees until I was able to pay him back. We worked out together which was a huge blessing in my life. It gave me the structure I desperately needed after prison and gave me something I could control. I could not control how the world saw me as a freshly released inmate, so until I was given a chance, this would be my focus.

To earn a few extra dollars my roommate suggested that I try selling plasma. I biked from Springfield to Arlington, via main street bridge. That is a long bike ride, but fortunately it was usually decent weather outside. Once I arrived and got to the kiosk to answer all the health questions I nearly fainted three times. I do not do well with health questionnaires I am forced to answer. I needed the money and I managed to plow through it. Fifty dollars seems small but it helped tremendously! Plasma donation was not a viable long term solution for income and I accepted it for what it was, a temporary financial relief.

After being out in the real world for about a month, I got a job interview at a subsidiary of a major medical company in town. The job title was Customer Service Representative earning thirteen dollars per hour, which was a good salary to start at. I interviewed and they loved me, I was their perfect candidate with prior experience. I was up front with them about my felonies and was given a start date and all the details about my first day. The start date was in late February, so I wasn't too excited about waiting a month when I was struggling financially. I was excited however to have this opportunity with a good paying job for getting back on my feet.

Two days before I was supposed to start in late February I got an email with a title that caught my attention. This email said my offer of employment was rescinded. I struggled financially my first six weeks out of prison and was so excited and to start this job and I WAS DEVASTATED. I had dealt with so much rejection from society in job applications and even using the gym at this point that I was sick. I felt that my only chance was slipping through my fingertips.

That same day I got the rejection notice, an old friend called from Melbourne and he wanted five pounds of weed and would break me off to be the middle man. I did not even flinch and I hung up on him immediately. I was NOT even wanting to toy with the idea of going back down that road again. Satan was certainly tempting with past mistakes when I was at my weakest, when toe nail clippers and other essentials were luxuries. Jesus had broken those chains in my life.

Pastor Steve had a contact at the Florida Times-Union, the local newspaper, and was able to get me a job. It started at minimum wage which was just over eight dollars per hour and worked twenty hours a week or less sometimes. It was a job and I was thankful for it. I was told by the Vice President of Production, Robert Todd, if I applied myself and worked hard that I could move up in the company. I was so very grateful for this opportunity, and I wasn't going to let them or myself down.

The job was difficult, I struggled and it was very strenuous work at times. The scheduling was all over the place, and I could never plan anything because of the erratic schedule. That work was nothing compared to some of the difficulties I faced in the chain gang though. I went to Pastor Steve to ask for grace because I could not afford to pay the one hundred dollar rent fee. I was shown grace by him similar to the graces Jesus shows us for our sins.

Once I had a job, I was moved to another ministry house on Boulevard St near 8th street in Springfield, and began attending First Baptist Church of Jacksonville. That would become my first church home outside of prison. I would bike from Springfield and felt loved and accepted there.

I became good friends with a man named Jimmy, a personal trainer at the YMCA. He gave me rides when I needed them and we joked around, hung out and talked for hours after I finished weightlifting. He went above and beyond his duties at the YMCA to become my friend when I really needed one.

After a while I moved to a house that Prisoners of Christ just purchased off of Myrtle Street. I was cleaning out my new room and again I was faced with great temptation. I saw five morphine pills when cleaning out my closet. I picked them up knowing exactly what they were and without hesitation I showed them to the house leader and we flushed them down the toilet. PRAISE GOD! In retrospect, I realized this was not good for our water system but it was the best possible choice on that day. That morning I was unable to read my daily devotional as I was helping another house member move in early that morning. When I went to read my devotional later that day it said:

1 Corinthians 10:13 (NIV)
No temptation has overtaken you except what is common to mankind. God is faithful; he will not let you be tempted beyond what you can bear. But when you are tempted, he will also provide a way out so that you can endure it.

God sent a message directly to me that day. Jesus had already broken the chains of addiction in my life and gave me the way out in that moment. There is power in the name of Jesus!

Months go by, and I continue working the night shift at Times-Union. I work hard, odd hours. I usually bike home from downtown to Myrtle street at 2 or 3AM. I pass all the dope boys and prostitutes along the way. I could see the ladies of the night from my bedroom window when I got home. Although I got plenty of flat tires back then, I am very thankful I never got one in the night heading home. I prayed for my safety and also those who were caught up in that life that I had been a part of for so long. I just hoped no one messed with me. I did have some close calls where people followed me though, and I was fortunate enough to lose them on my bicycle.

Eventually I managed to save barely enough money to move out on my own. Jack was released from prison and came back to the neighborhood. We decided to get a place together in Riverside. He got a job, enrolled in school and he was putting all his effort into bettering his life. It was amazing to see what addicts are capable of doing when they are clean and sober. We looked at several different apartments and were rejected numerous times because of our felonies. Neither of us had violent or sexual charges but people did not want to give felons a chance. After more searching we finally found a place that would accept us just across from the John Gorrie condos. It was close to where Stockton and Myra streets meet, and I was one block away from my buddy Jimmy so I was excited.

Two days after I moved in my buddy Jimmy was found dead in his house. I was there when the police kicked down his door and found him. It was an ominous way to start my time in that neighborhood. I was deeply saddened by this loss of amazing creative life. I sought peace in Memorial Park that night and many times after. At his funeral, they read a poem he had written called "God's Lighthouse", and he was truly a beacon of light for God in the darkness I encountered early on. Although we knew each other all of 6 months, he made a profound impact on my life.

I struggled financially but I was happy. I was in a place that was vibrant and full of life close to my job. I could bike anywhere I needed to go and was blessed with one of the prettiest commutes in all of Jacksonville. I did not have to deal with traffic or parking and it was a simple seven minute bike ride to work. I could easily bike to the Riverside Publix but my budget often required Walmart which was a bit more difficult. Memorial Park became a place where I spent a great deal of time because I enjoyed it so. The park was free to all so I could just sit there and enjoy it while reading a book or taking photos on my cell phone. It was interesting to see the different angles of the Life statue and how It plays with the rest of the park.

Originally, I had moved into the house with just some blankets to use as a mattress because I could not afford a bed. I was very thankful to find an old mattress in the trash a quarter mile down the street. I dragged it all the way home where I had to cross Stockton street which was full of traffic. I cleaned it up as best as I could and used it for a while until I could afford a new mattress. It took me months to save up for my first big purchase, a new mattress. Some may think of how gross that is, that I would take a mattress from the trash. But it sure beat laying on a hardwood floor. It is all about perspective and being thankful for what you have!

Jack decided to get back together with his girlfriend Lisa who he used drugs with in the past. They both claimed to be clean when they got back together but within a week they relapsed and began smoking crack again. I got a few text messages one night while working production at the Times- Union asking when I would be home. It seemed as though they were hiding something and their behavior became increasingly erratic. I received a letter from my landlord who gave us notice that we had three days until we would be evicted. Wait, what? I paid my rent! My roommate took my money and smoked it instead of paying the rent. Then he created stories as to why we got the evection notice and told me not to worry about it. I found a letter on my table one evening after getting home late from work, explaining how sorry he was and he could NOT pay his part of the rent and he stole my money for the rent. I had twenty-four hours until the rent was due with zero savings and no way to get fast cash. In that desperate moment all I could do was pray.

That next morning I felt completely helpless and I read my daily devotional. It was **Phillipians 4:6-7 Don't worry about anything; instead, pray about everything. Tell God what you need, and thank him for all he has done. Then you will experience God's peace, which exceeds anything we can understand. His peace will guard your hearts and minds as you live in Christ Jesus.** This verse gave me peace. I knew that everything would be ok. I prayed, and God opened doors I would have never seen. Someone who barely knew me at the time paid my electric bill to keep that going in my name. My dad was able to cover my rent until I could pay him back. That is something I was so skeptical about, but God allowed that relationship to grow again before and after this incident. I struggled, sure. But through this storm, God showed me that I needed to trust Him, when I felt helpless, as

I can do nothing without Him. **Psalm 56:3 (NIV) When I am afraid, I put my trust in you.**

I applied myself at work consistently and was given a promotion at the Times Union, shipping and receiving team leader. The new hours were seven in the morning till four in the afternoon. I finally did not have to work the night shift and I now had a sunrise commute along the riverwalk as I was still not able to have a divers license. Most people would have considered this to be a true hardship, but I saw it as an opportunity. The bike ride in to work was a quick seven minutes and I was able to see the beautiful sunrise along the riverwalk almost every day while getting in some cardio. I recognized how the urban core of town was incredibly beautiful. I started taking photos on my cell phone of the sunrises on the river and downtown in the background. I do not understand how any-

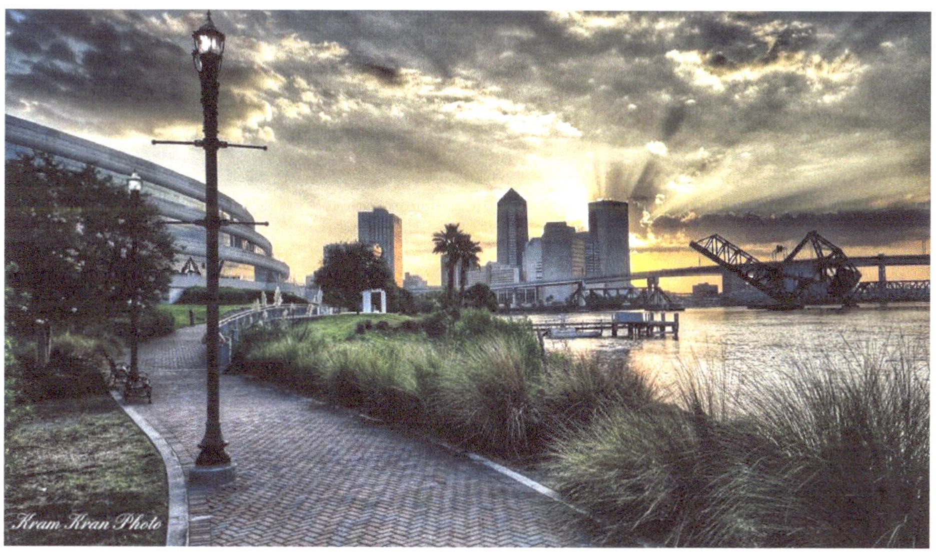

"Jogging through Sunshine" One of Mark's early
photographic favorites, taken on his way into work
along Jacksonville's riverwalk, September 2015

one could not possibly love our riverwalk with the magnificent view of downtown.

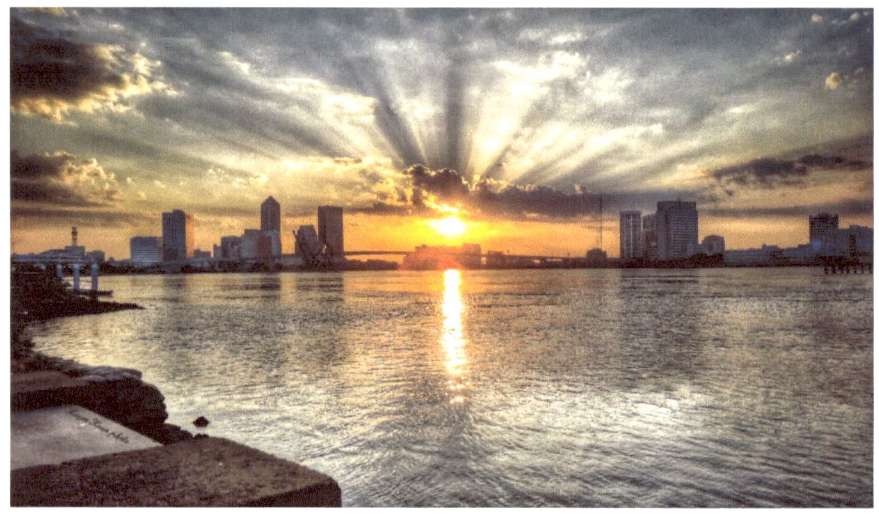

"Divine Duval" taken on his way into work along
Jacksonville's riverwalk, September 2015

12. Bob

There were not too many people on the Times-Union day shift in production, but one was a man by the name of Bob. He was the chief of security and the only security present during the day. When I got to work after a great sunrise I would quickly edit my photos in Snapseed, a free app used for photo editing that I highly recommend. For anyone who is interested in photography, it is a great beginning to learn the concepts that help create your own style. I showed my edited photos to everyone I could find who was willing to look at them. Bob always deeply enjoyed my shots. I also shared them with friends and various groups on Facebook where they would get a lot of appreciation. This encouraged my passion on a deeper level as people I did not even know appreciated my work. I had no extra money at the time and I could barely afford the cheap phone I was using. The saying goes, "The best camera is the one you have on you!"

I was not able to drive at the time and had to ride my bike to get anywhere. Bob began giving me rides to the store after he saw me biking and carrying ten bags of groceries on my handlebars. He gave me rides to Walmart or anywhere I needed to go. He never complained because all he wanted to do was help. He liked photography so I showed him Snapseed. He enjoyed my photos and wanted to help me grow in my love for photography. I think Bob just truly loves helping people find what they love.

Bob blessed me with one of his cameras, a Nikon D7000 with an 18-135mm Nikkor lens, a mid-grade "prosumer" camera. A truly wonderful camera that could do so much more than my phone ever could. We took trips to shoot photos and enjoy time out in the city. I learned the basics of photography including shooting in manual and raw modes. Bob's patience and generosity paid off and I greatly appreciate everything he has done for me. Over time he has become one of my closest friends.

I packed that camera in my backpack and would ride my bike along the riverwalk whenever I thought there was a chance of a decent sunrise. No matter the whether-rain, oppressive heat, or freezing wind and cold I was riding the bicycle heading to work. I got to understand nature and appreciated it first hand no matter what was coming at me.

Bob's fascination with art and photography, along with knowledge of the art world, helped me immensely to grow as an artist. When I landed my very first artist exhibit at the downtown Jacksonville Library, Bob not only helped me figure out my themes for the show, but also helped me get the canvases printed and the hanging wire applied. With the stress of getting back in school, getting the exhibit prepared and stress from work I came down with Bell's Palsy. I could not physically smile at my own artist reception and I had to tape my eyes shut at night because I could not close them. It was Bob who drove me to the doctor and then the emergency room without asking for anything in return from me. That was a foreign concept to me as everyone in my life only wanted to help if it was for their own gain.

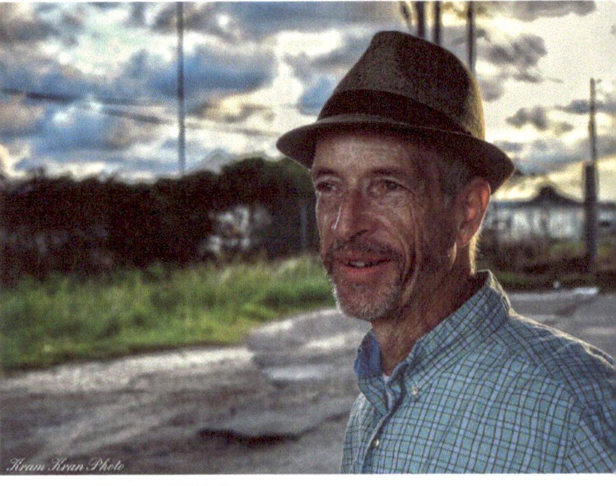

Bob, 2015

Bob is a great example of putting others needs ahead of their own and I love his spirit of helpfulness. He is a part of our family and was a groomsman in my wedding. Over the past few years we have gone on many adventures and trips together. He has contributed countless hours to helping me in life and helping me with my passion and business with photography. Bob has shown me what a true friend is and I am forever grateful for him.

During this time I saw the work of a photographer Matt Bluejay on Facebook and I reached out to him for questions dealing with photography. He was very patient in helping me learn my own editing style with my photos. There were several photographers who I thought produced great work but he was on a different level. When I saw a photo he took outside of the Times Union building by the riverwalk I made it my goal to take quality photos like that. If he could do it I could find my own way to do it.

The other photographic style I appreciated was the Time Union photographer Bob Self (not my buddy Bob I have described previously). Bob Self had a way of seeing photos and telling stories visually that were far more appealing to me than any other photos in the paper. Since I worked at the Times-Union I read the newspaper almost every day on my break. Instantly I could tell which photos were Bob Self's just by his style. I longed to have that sort of quality and visual branding.

My Buddy Bob's friendship has been a true blessing in our family. Although we have both moved on from the Times-Union, we still are very much a part of each other's lives. I enjoy seeing the creative photos he comes up with and shares. We have been doing that for almost 5 years now and it never gets old.

13. A Man of God

Steve Clifton has always been a man of God in my eyes. When I walked into the Prisoners of Christ ministry housing, he was busy discipling George. I was sweaty because it was hot and I just finished a long bike ride home. I was so surprised that this man was taking the time to invest in us ex-cons when most of society wanted nothing to do with us. I hit the shower so quickly after that bike ride so I could join them for their time together. He was actively applying God's Word to George's life, and mine as well.

The next time Steve showed up George was not at the house because they had some kind of miscommunication. I asked to be discipled by Steve as well and he gladly worked me in to his busy schedule. We began what would be a year and a half of weekly discipleship and we became good friends. I went through several rough storms in my life and Steve showed me what God's word said about it and how to apply it to my situation. Steve walked with me week by week through discipleships while leading me on the path of sanctification.

Steve started to consider me part of the family as he knew I did not have much family. It was one of the greatest gifts God has ever given to me, a loving family to be a part of. Steve always showed humility and love to all those around him and has been a tremendous positive influence in my life. He truly leads by his example. He was never too busy or disinterested. He never bragged, unless his Tennessee Vols won a football game.

It was through Steve Clifton, a senior pastor at First Baptist Church of Jacksonville, that I got involved with the church on a regular basis. This was a life changing journey over the next few years. Eventually, Steve would be the pastor presiding over my wedding.

The church had a reputation of being the rich or high society church in Jacksonville. I had to ride my bike to church and would arrive covered in sweat during the summer time. I did not have money for fancy clothes and would wear shorts and a t-shirt on a regular basis. Steve always welcomed me with open arms and never made me feel bad about my appearance. In fact he praised me for it using my situation as an example of faith no matter what hardships may come someones way. I never felt anything but acceptance from him and most of the people at First Baptist Church.

There has been a repeat of Godly men named Steve in my life. Steven Kelley, my friend behind bars who encouraged me to grow in my walk with the Lord. Pastor Steve McCoy of Prisoners of Christ did many wonderful things for men coming out of prison. Steve Clifton brought me into his family and Steve Schnell who helped immensely when times got dark. I cannot thank them enough for all that they have done for me over the years. I call this group of men the "Godly Steves".

14. Learning Logistics

During my days as a druggy I tried school for a few semesters. I had too much craziness going on in my life and the drug deals and partying kept getting in the way. In the last few weeks of my incarceration at the Jacksonville Bridges there was a career fair of sorts. I met Deborah Ayer who helped guide me after my release on how to get back into school. After some false starts I successfully started my courses at Florida State College at Jacksonville.

We sat down and discussed what professional careers can a felon succeed in. I already had experience in shipping and receiving from a previous job so I was encouraged to peruse a degree in logistics. Jacksonville is known as the logistics capital of America so I figured it could be a good fit.

One of the classes I had to take involved a field trip to a warehouse on the westside of town. I was still biking to the FSCJ downtown campus so biking to the westside of town after work was almost impossible. I asked my college professor if he knew someone I could hitch a ride with and he offered me a ride with him. While driving out to the warehouse I explained my past and why I was on a bicycle. He told me he had a very similar past which he overcame only by the power of Jesus Christ transforming him into the man he is now. He has held some important positions on campus and became an author where he told his testimony and God's love for him. He was an inspiration to me as a real world example of someone overcoming their past, using it for God's glory and being a positive influence on people lives.

I enjoyed learning about the business end of logistics and how it transforms our world at every level. I also got certified in a new eight track logistics course that was offered by the Council of Supply Chain Management Professionals, a governing body of logistics. I became one of the first three graduates of that certification program while at Florida State College at Jacksonville.

After more than two years I managed to earn my Bachelor degree in Logistics and Supply Chain Management. I know it made my dad very happy to know I finally, after 14 years, finally finished my degree. It was still incredibly difficult to find a job as a felon. Even six years later that conviction still haunted me in very visible ways. In our information age it is so easy for someone to use that information against you. I was turned down for multiple jobs simply because of a felony on my record. I finally found a job in logistics that God had prepared for me all along. Once I quit trying to do things my way the Lord opened up doors for me that I did not even knock on. It has been a huge blessing to walk with Him and see His power. Like the saying goes, "Let go and let God".

15. Kiss and Makeup

In January 2015 Laurie Clifton, Steve Clifton's wife, mentioned that she wanted me to participate in the church's annual passion play. I had a few things going on with work and the gym but I was not overly busy. I was still hesitant because it was quite a large time commitment. It involved three-hour practices four or five times a week. Laurie made the comment, "You never know. God may have the perfect woman for you there in the play!" While I was certainly interested before, I believe that was the tipping argument I needed to serve.

Months of preparation go into the event, and we begin in early February rehearsing for our roles. I was a disciple in the passion play. Although I did not have a speaking role, it was defi-

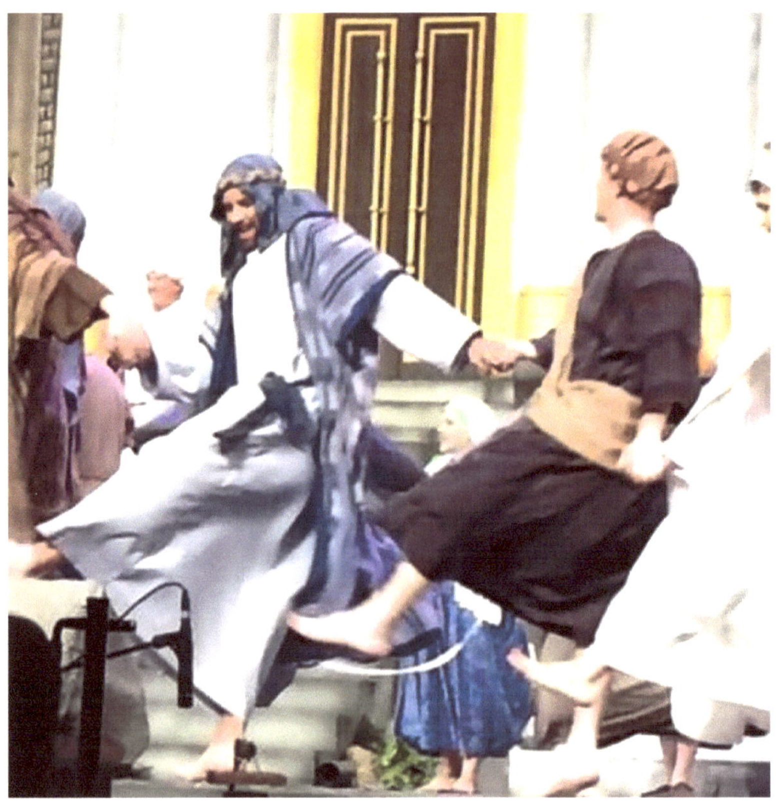

Mark on stage at First Baptist Church of Jacksonville's 2015 Passion Play

nitely a very intense position for me to play. I do not consider myself a thespian in the least bit. But I was honored to serve. As the dress rehearsals started, I saw one of "Herod's Hoes" as they are called. She was beautiful, in costume and with long curly hair. I noticed her a few more times, like the first time I saw her in one scene where we are walking with Jesus through the city of Jerusalem. I reached out to make my hand connect with hers, and then went about my role in the performance.

God had a plan. The lady who caught my eye during the rehearsal served elsewhere in the passion play as well. Kristin was my makeup artist the next day and throughout the remainder of the performances. We got to talking, and became friends instantly. We talked every day pretty much non stop. It was simple with her and we had a wonderful connection. Our first date and picture together was at Memorial Park where we drank coffee and walked along the balustrades. She didn't care that I did not have any money. As I like to say, she brought the coffee and I brought the park.

Kristin has the distinction of being the first person to hire me as a family photographer. I loved seeing how she was such caring mother to her boys. I fell in love with this sweet woman

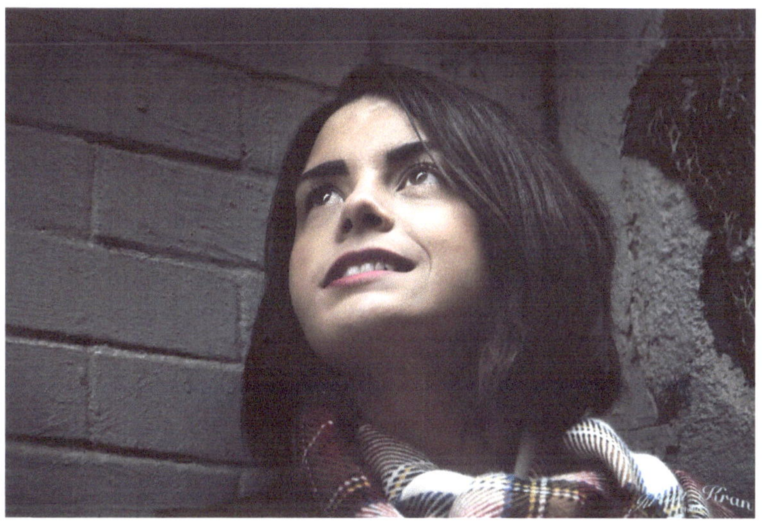

Kristin, January 2017

who loved her family and looked past my shortcomings. At that point, I was still a complete novice with the camera but she enjoyed my company and the photos. We went on many more dates around Jacksonville, including many more dates at Memorial Park. A little over a year later on July 4, 2016, as the fireworks went off along the beach, I asked her to be my wife. She said Yes!

We decided to get married on October 20, 2017. I wanted at least one of us to have graduated from college, and I was finishing up my bachelor's degree in the summer of 2017. As the wedding date grew closer, one of the groomsmen who knew my financial situation asked "Mark, how are you going to pay for this wedding?" I replied, "I just have to have faith that the Lord will provide." We did not have an extravagant or expensive wedding by most standards but covering the basics of a wedding would be a challenge for me. We were praying that many of my photographs in the airport exhibit would sell to be sure we could cover my costs for the weddings. Some did, but God would provide in unforeseen ways. Ways that our finite minds cannot begin to comprehend the power our Infinite God possesses.

16. Friends behind the gates

It is a sad truth that many of my friends I met behind the gates have been released only to go back right back behind bars. George was a friend who got baptized with me at First Baptist church and within his first two years of being free he relapsed and went back to prison. He died in prison after he pawned a stolen gun. George knew it was illegal for a felon to own a firearm therefor I believe he became hopeless and did it to himself. Originally he was in prison for several decades and maybe he became institutionalized on some level. Seeing a man love life so much only to go back to such a dark place is truly heart breaking for me.

One of my dear friends who I affectionally call a member of " the Godly Steves" is back behind bars for an attempted murder charge. God used this man in miraculous ways behind bars to bring me and many others to church. He was a great encouragement to many to be stronger in our workouts and faith and stronger. Anger can be a real demon and can ultimately cause people to do crazy things and ruin their lives.

Freddy, one of my closest friends, whose paintings of landscapes and seascapes was some of the first art I truly appreciatcd, is also in prison for a few years. This man is a great artist and I look forward to the day he is free again.

When coming to the Prisoners of Christ ministry a person has to be on the buddy system for two weeks. Everywhere you go, someone from the ministry has to accompany you. A guy was released from the buddy system and the very first time he went somewhere by himself he failed. He ended up violating probation at a crack house and was sent back to prison.

I have been saddened to see people fall again and again. It saddens me, to see their lives wasted from poor choices. Some have not had a change of heart, but then other times I see those who have had a change of heart get frustrated after months of getting no where and slip back into drugs and alcohol. Once there, it is a slippery slope. I am thoroughly convinced that if I ever pick up alcohol or drugs again, I am on a one way trip back to prison. It might not be that day or that month, but one thing will lead to another and my addictions will get the best of me.

I am not saying any of these men are guilty or innocent, but I am saying that we, as a society, set men and women who get out of prisons up for failure. Lives are lost and wasted, whether out of desperation, survival, anger, or a number of other reasons. We as a society need to do more to prepare people for the job market who have been inside for years. They get out and have few skills, and have a high chance of failing, going back on taxpayer's dime instead of living their fullest potential and contributing to society. But what good is it if you cannot get a job that pays your bills? What good is it if you cannot get decent housing out of a high crime neighborhood when you have little or no resources? Why do apartments tell me they have a 99 year grace period on allowing felons to apply for housing, especially when they are marketed to help low income families?

As a society we need to do more to prepare people for life once they are out from behind bars. People who have been incarcerated longer need more help than people with a shorter sentence. People who have just been released have few skills, little credible employment, no support system of any value and have a high chance of failing and going back to prison.

According to the Institute of Justice, incarceration costs an average of more than thirty-one thousand dollars per inmate, per year, nationwide. In America, almost two and a half million people are in prison. Taxpayers pay upwards of eighty-one **BILLION** dollars to house people in prison. It is much better and cheaper for society to have people rehabilitated and giving them a chance to live an honest life rather than in prison.

Think about the money that would be put back into the economy with even a small fraction of the people back in the free world. What can we do to help felons so they do not have to go back and cost taxpayers money?

I have an ongoing photographic project that received a micro-grant from the Cultural Council of Greater Jacksonville and the Community First CARES Foundation. Visually I show some-

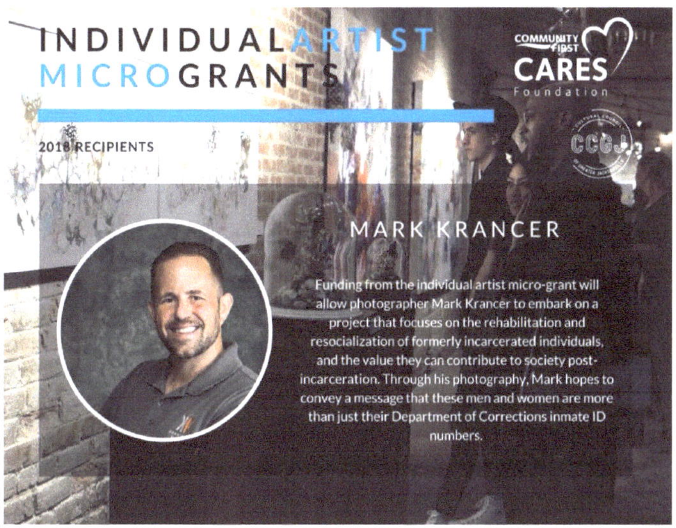

one who has been incarcerated in the past and include how they contribute to society in the free world. Whether through their education, their family, their job, or volunteer work, these previously incarcerated individuals help make our world a better place. If someone is interested in learning more about this project please reach out to me for more information. For someone who is just getting out, a small opportunity provided by someone who had a change of heart may help save their life.

17. Life In The River

On September 10th and 11th, 2017, Hurricane Irma battered
Florida. During that time, I was fully prepared to "hunker down"
and ride out the storm. The Sunday afternoon that Irma was
coming, my friend called me up asking if i wanted to ride
around. Since I had my preparations fully done, I said sure
why not. My inquisitive mind can get the best of me sometimes. He picked me up, and we rode out to the beach. As we
head down A1A, we stop at a friend's beach house. This is the
beach house where I had proposed to Kristin the year before.
We get out, and the wind is stinging us with wet sand. We
could barely stand at my friend's house, the wind was so
strong. We then journeyed down to St. Augustine, and made it
over the bridge about an hour before they closed.

I saw Kristin and her family down in St. Augustine, and then
my friend and I went back to Jacksonville. There are little
things that aren't thought about on a regular basis that become very deadly under the right circumstances. The power
went out on I95, and a tree fell early, and onto the road. It took
up the right lane of the north-bound 95. It was completely
dark, and we were driving about 50mph. We had just happened to switch into the middle lane about a minute before the
tree, but we did not see the tree until it was entirely too late. If
we had not have just happened to get in that middle lane, we
would have slammed into a tree at 50mph in a hurricane. That
obviously would not be an ideal circumstance, and one entirely of our doing. Not the smartest decision I ever made.

The next morning, once the rain stopped, I started looking
outside. the wind was howling, and the water was rising. I did
not have TV in my house, so i was unsure about tides and was
not seeing a lot of storm coverage, other than on google and
Facebook. But I had a creek behind my house near CoRk Arts
District. I kept watching it rise and rise and rise. I was concerned, and ended up moving my car a bit. I settled into one of

my books (about photography of course) and was just passing time.

Then my phone dings, with a text message.

My pastor and a father figure, Steve Clifton, texts me "They're telling people to get out in memorial park with 4 more feet of storm surge coming in from the river cresting. Be safe. The statue you took pictures of in park is getting flooded at base of bronze. So the globe will be under 4 feet of water.

my reply: "Oh wow. I gotta get a pic of that!!"

From that point on, at 10:37am on September 11th, I was out there. The wind was still blowing hard, but the rain stopped. I could take photos with my gear. I got in the car, and figure I will ride down Riverside Ave. That was not happening! I was going down Stockton street, and I couldn't go much further than Herschel Street. Oak and Riverside ave were completely flooded. I was just blown away. I knew Riverside flooded, but I was really not prepared for that moment. There is a hill going down Herschel that also was completely flooded. I was looking around, taking photos there. At that point, I knew I had to photograph the impact of the storm as much as possible. I saw my friend Shaun out there on his bicycle. We spoke for a few minutes, and parted ways, him biking to Memorial Park and me driving. I had to go up several streets and back track down to Memorial Park.

Once I got out of the car on Margaret street, I realized I could not cross the street at the regular crossing spot without getting wet. I think, during events like this, you have to have that critical moment of thinking: is this worth me getting my clothes wet over? Once I crossed that line, I was in. I walked over to memorial park, and instantly saw the huge surge that Irma had brought to the park. There was more grey and brown than green that day from the water.

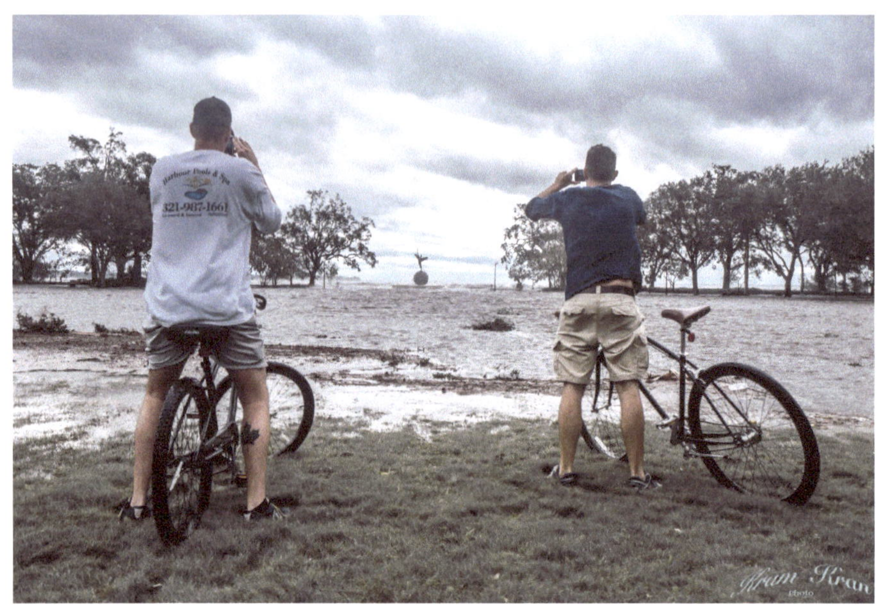

The first scene Mark saw as he entered Memorial park on
September 11th, 2017.

I saw Shaun and his friend shortly after arriving. They began
getting in the water. And I started to "get my feet wet" so to
speak. I started taking photos from way back, and i was getting some cool photos, but not what I envisioned. I knew from
several years of photographing the park that I prefer a side
angle instead of a straight on shot of "Life", composition wise.
So i approached from the right side of the park, and was
steadily walking around in knee-deep or slightly higher water.
with my lens being a 18-135mm Nikkor, I wanted to get the
statue in a full, but balanced frame, as a wave crashed over it.
I wanted to get the spray washing over the statue. I had the
vision, but I could not achieve it yet.

After seeing Shaun and his friend take the plunge, I decided I
needed to as well. I decided against putting my phone up on
the higher land. My old life leads me to not trust doing things

like that, even in the middle of a storm. I start wading into waist deep water, in my finest pair of sandals. I took my car keys out of my pocket, as i did not want the key fob to get wet. it's interesting to realize how modern life keeps us full of stuff to carry around with us, especially when it needs to be above the waist. I had my camera, my keys, and my phone. 3 pieces of electronics, 3 pieces that do not like water. I placed my key fob in my mouth, with the plastic portion of my YMCA tag being clenched in my teeth. I placed the phone in my left hand, with the belt clip. I held the camera in my right hand, firing the shutter off with my index finger. I had to adjust the lens with the few fingers i had free from my left hand, which was otherwise holding the cell phone. You could say my hands were full, and my modern day "Life" was in my hands.

Following Shaun and his friend out to the base of the statue resulted in a series of photos that capture the park in an entirely different light than usual, and have shown the power of nature. Photographs of that sequence have been shared locally and nationally, even as far as being in a *National Geographic* essay about climate change. There were other people that went out to the base of the statue. One guy, who I talked to after he ventured to the base of the statue, mentioned he had been shocked when he touched the base of the statue. Fortunately he was physically ok, but it had taken him by surprise.

I knew the instant I took the photo, I got what I wanted. I just hoped it turned out right from a technical perspective, which I could not really check until later. The viewfinder gave me an idea of what I got, but until I got home and started looking at the photo on the computer I couldn't be sure. Really I had wanted to get close enough to show the water droplets spraying over "Life". That was my goal. And sometimes the combination of elements, especially during severe weather, need to line up just right. Composition and exposure can be difficult enough under regular conditions, but when the wind is howling and you have debris in the water, downed power lines around you, and rapidly changing compositions, it can be much more

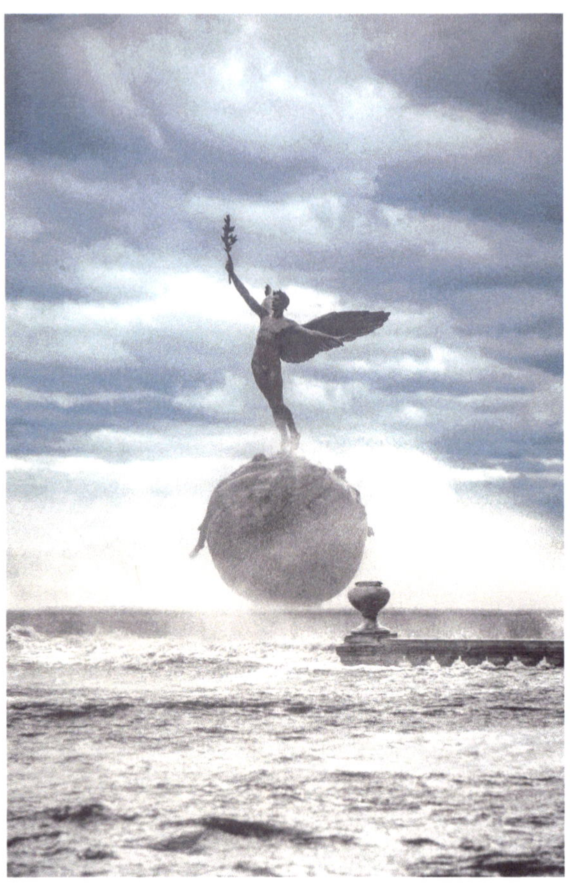

"Life In The River" by Mark Krancer

difficult to gauge in the field. I took approximately 300 photos that morning, and I got "the one". There was something about the way the wave crashed at the base of the statue's feet that just became very symbolic. It is a beautiful and inspiring statue on a regular day, but it took on a whole new meaning for me that day. For those who are interested, the technical components of the shot are Nikon D7000 with a Nikkor 18-135mm lens at 105mm. Shutter speed is 1/800th of a second, F5.6, and ISO 280. I wanted the shutter speed to be fast enough so to freeze the wave's water droplets as it crashed over the "Life" statue.

I continued taking photos. This incredible, hopefully once-in-a-lifetime event was amazing to view. I don't mean that in a way to downplay the destruction that many people received that day, but just that this storm was taking scenes that were part of my daily commute, such as the riverwalk, and transforming them by the power of this water. I went down familiar territory, following the road and seeing familiar scenes in a completely different view. The parking lot at my gym, the Winston YMCA, was flooded for the majority of it's lower level. I stopped by my work, Florida Times-Union, and noticed waves crashing and McCoy's creek about to overtake the parking lot. Large chunks, 4 feet or more, of the cement were broken off.

 I parked at Times-Union and ventured along the now hostile territory between Times-Union and Haskell. The waves were breaking over the river walk, completely drenching me as I took photos of the action. I had to time my walking in between

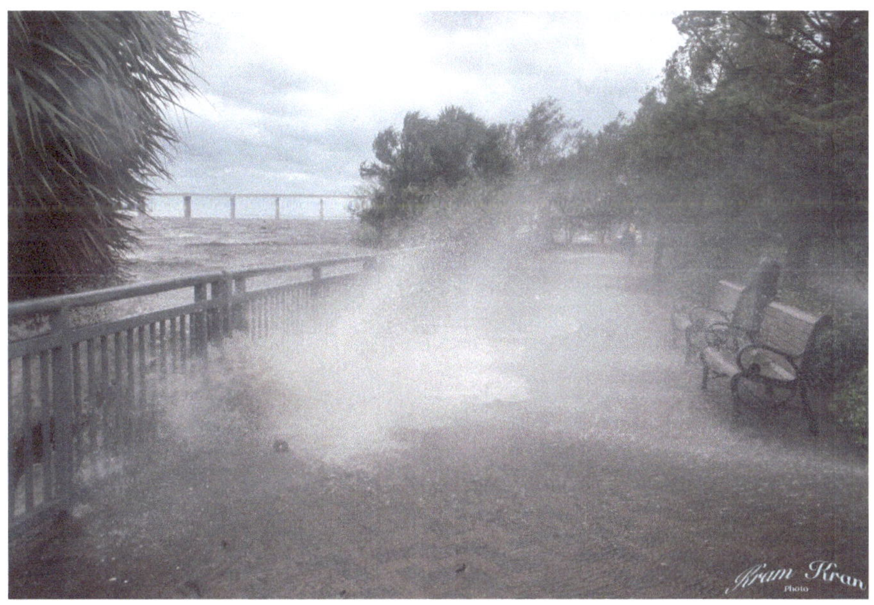

Waves crashing on the Northbank riverwalk between the old Times-Union building and the Haskell Building, September 11th, 2017.

the waves crashing, so as not to get myself and my gear soaked in the process.

I managed to get over to Haskell, and the dock was completely underwater. All I could see was the pilings, and the top portion of the gate. The ferocity of the river had overtaken the day. Waves crash over the same walk where I peacefully recorded so many beautiful sunrises early on in my photographic career. It was very intense to feel the power of God in the St. John's River, making sure I did not get washed away by it. Waves continued to crash, and one even managed to hit

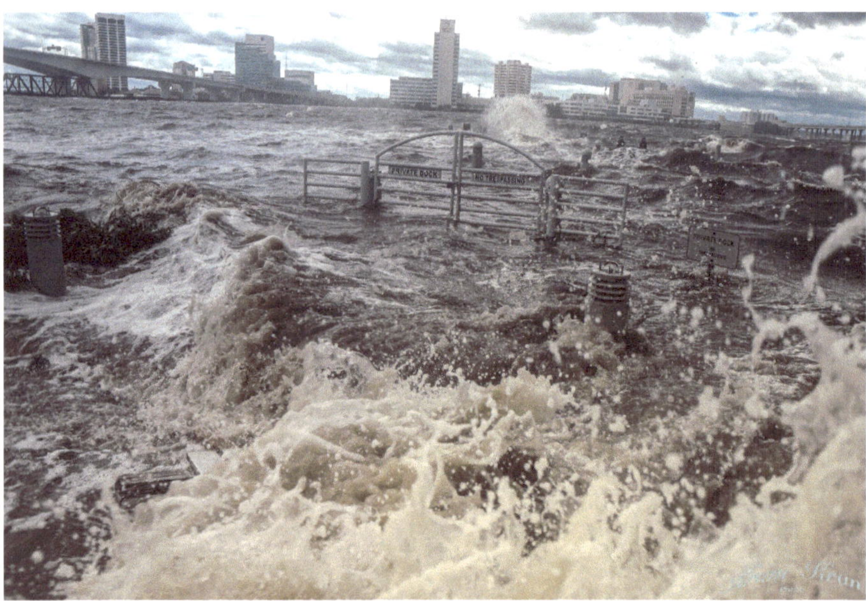

the lens and the camera. By that point there was not a dry piece of cloth on me. I knew I had to continue shooting, because there was not much else I could do about it at that point. I didn't leave the house immediately after a hurricane prepared in the least bit. Sandals and not even a plastic bag to cover the camera. I was so excited to shoot and didn't want to miss the action, I couldn't be distracted by something as trivial as hurricane preparation! (haha)

My friends Tony and Bob were with me, and we ventured into San Marco. As we went over the Fuller Warren bridge and saw San Marco from above, the ground below had no streets. It was just water everywhere, and the rooftop of buildings visible. We ended up going down to Phillips Highway, and making our way back into San Marco. My thought had been to get to the lions statue in the middle of San Marco square. With water everywhere, there was no way I was getting close to that. Everything was blocked off. We park, and get walking. I end up by Hendricks and La Salle. people in kayaks are passing through traffic intersections.

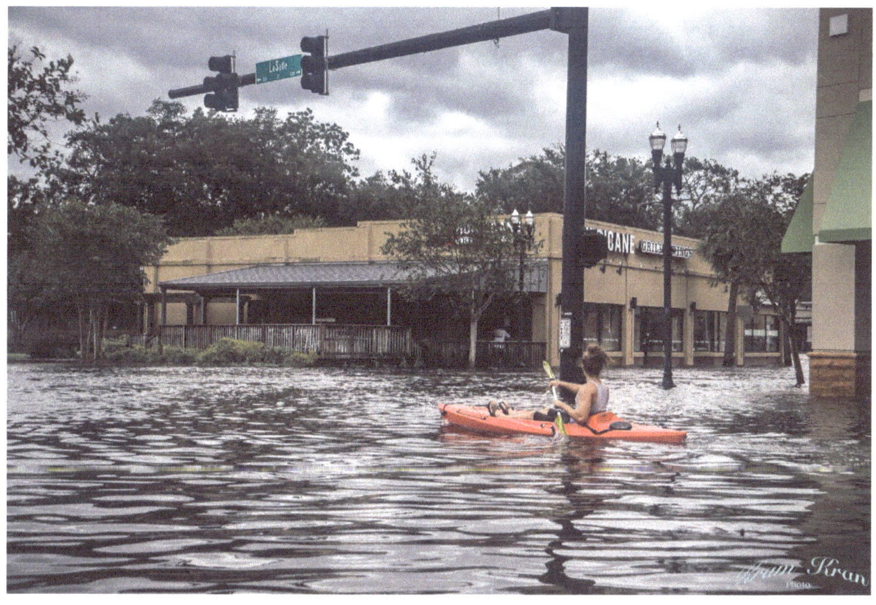

I watch this family get saved by first responders in a boat. They are evacuated from their flooded house to dry land. I try getting photos, but my lens fogs up at that point. It would have been a perfect shot. But as the first responders save the family, one of them yells to me "watch out for manhole covers, they come up from the ground and you can fall down in them, we will never find you!" I had never thought about manhole covers. It had just not crossed my mind. I told this to Tony, who says "yeah, when you see bubbles coming up out of the road, thats when you know a manhole cover has come up." I start shuffling through the water as slowly as I can. As soon as I see bubbles coming up out of the middle of the road, thats when I know where I draw the line. I turned around and slowly proceeded the way I had come. I didn't make it very far in San Marco!

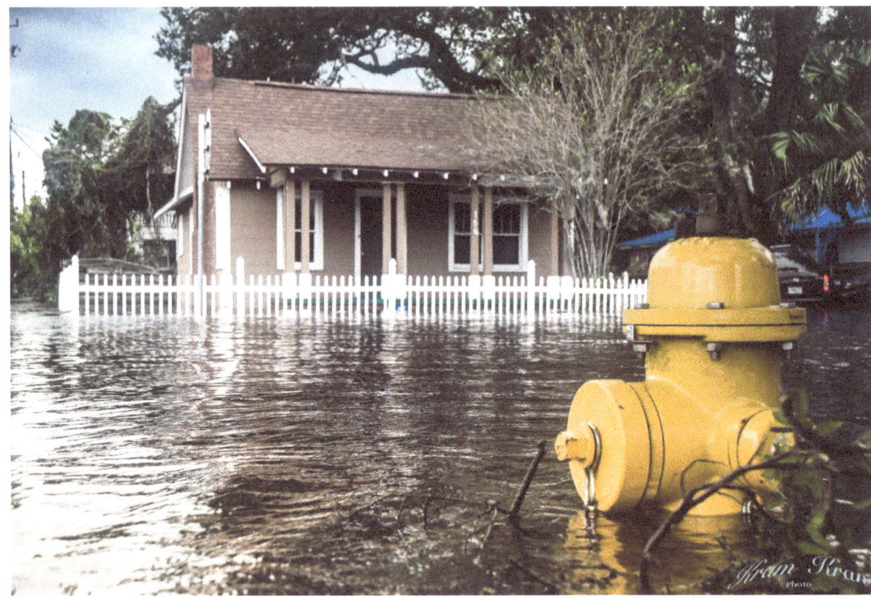

Tony, Bob, and I part ways. I went into downtown Jacksonville. Water street was very literal that day. I go up to Forsyth and work my way down Laura towards the landing. I continue into waist-deep water around the circle with the Andrew Jackson statue, just amazed at the power. Whole blocks are submerged, and I am blown away by it. I go down by the landing, and the streets are submerged, the Andrew Jackson statue is just standing in the middle of it all. People are splashing around everywhere, but the river is reminding everyone around that it is in control of the day. I snap some photos, and head back to the car. By this point, I have been out in the hurricane elements for about 4 hours and I'm soaked from constantly being in the water or splashed by waves. I need to chill for a minute.

I head back to the house, which somehow never lost power. I suppose I am on the hospital's power grid. I shower quickly, then I start looking at these photos I got. As I view the photos of Memorial Park, I am seeing so many that are close, but don't quite get exactly what I was looking for. Either water sprays up on the lens, or the angle, composition, or timing is off. I edit a round of photos, and start posting them. I am blown away with what I had, but I kept looking through the raw photos some more. Then I see the frame, which becomes "Life In The River". The composition is really what I envisioned, so I take a few minutes to edit this and make sure it is as perfect as I can get it. Some people accused me of photoshopping this image, but I assure you it is not. It is edited in lightroom, de-hazed and some color changes to make it more appealing to my palette. But nothing is "photoshopped" in or out of the image, other than minor spot healing.

Before I found this composition, I had already uploaded a photo or two to facebook, the Jacksonville photography meet up group, with the title "Life In The River". I thought It was a fitting title, considering the "Life" statue was indeed IN the St. Johns river that day. Could I have come up with something more amazing? Poetic, reflective of the day? perhaps. But It would have taken me a long time, and time was not on my side. I was editing these photos and uploading them as quickly as possible for a few reasons:

1) I was unsure if I would lose power at any point
2) I felt a responsibility to get photos out of this craziness as quickly as possible
3) I had to get these shots taken care and uploaded so I could go back and shoot towards sunset.

I was so excited and not really thinking about the symbolic enormity that photo would possess. But I knew this was to be the best of my photos to come out of that day, so I renamed that photo immediately to "Life In The River" on facebook, and posted it to a few groups.

I go back out into the flooded streets towards sunset. Sunset is my favorite time to photograph. Especially after all the rain, there may have been an amazingly dynamic sunset. After Hurricane Dorian in 2019, we had an amazing purple sky. I did not get a sunset that night, but I got something amazing and powerful in another way.

When I first went out to Memorial Park on that day, the river was so high that I could not see anything below the base of the statue. And I was honestly just so blown away by the power of the river that I never really even thought of the balustrade. Maybe I had a passing moment, but nothing of deep contemplation I can recall.

When I got back to Memorial Park towards sunset, the water had receded considerably. High tide had been over for several hours, and Irma had passed by the evening. So I go back to the park, and I see a good crowd out by the statue. As I approach, I start to notice there is no balustrade wall left in areas that normally separate the park from the river. Then I see people are walking all over the balustrades, which have fallen

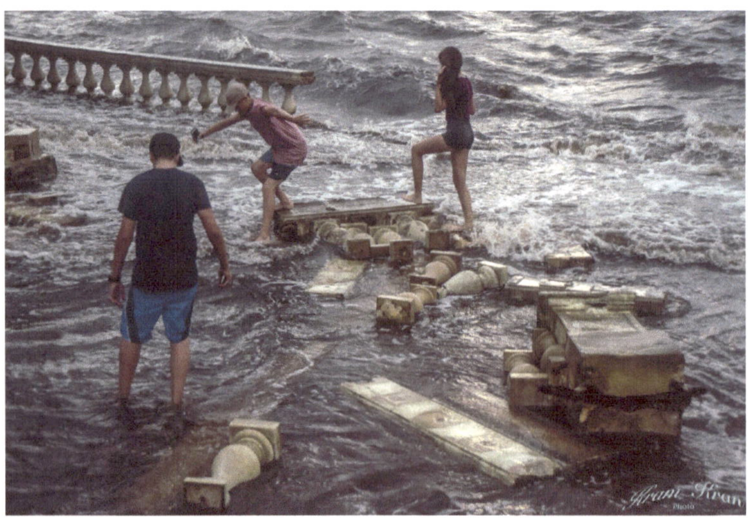

over as though fallen chess pieces. It appeared almost as though it was a lost ruins of ancient Greece or Rome, except displaced in modern Jacksonville.

The water level by this point was where typically the ground stops. So, as you looked towards the river, especially in the places without the balustrade, you literally could not see where the end of the land was and where the falloff to the river actually began.

Memorial Park was the first park I ever truly enjoyed. Some of my first photos I took as a photographer were along the balustrades, of the balustrades, even over the balustrades (I have a photo of me with a selfie stick held over the balustrade, but I was not using it for a selfie!) Kristin and I had our first date in that park. By this point, every 10 minutes or so when I would stop to look down at my phone, I had 200+ notifications on my phone about people liking, commenting, or sharing my photos. I knew I had captured something special. But at the same time I had this immense sadness come over me about the state of my beloved park. I felt a responsibility, as some-one who loves the park. I can't just be an observer, I had to participate. It was at that point I said that I will use this photo to help the park however it can.

"Life In The River" was like nothing I had ever experienced as far as a photo going viral. I shared it to originally 9 facebook pages within the first 4 hours. From there, I know it had to have over 10,000 shares. One man, Jason Braddock, shared the photo from the Memorial Park Association's page and had over 2,700 shares just from his post. I roughly estimate that a million people viewed the photo on facebook around the world. I think I may have had photos on pages get 50 shares before, but the sheer power of how those photos spread was almost as powerful, in my mind, as the very storm that these photos covered.

I figure there may be several reasons as to why the photo got so much attention, along with the others I posted. For one, it is a wonderful photo. It symbolized the triumph of Life over the storms that come our way. It is a good symbolic gesture of faith, hope, and Life. But it also was put on facebook quickly, by that afternoon, when people were scanning for any coverage of the storm. My quick facebook photo album was beating major coverage by news media outlets. With so many people having their power out in their house, they may have been bored or just scrolling for information however they could. And the photos could tell the visual story, very early on, about how Jacksonville was doing.

Facebook made that photo what it became. If facebook had not been around, the photo would have had some recognition, but it would not have had the widespread attention it received. I had that photo up before many media companies could even post their stories. I have had many people from Jacksonville come up to me and say that when they think of Hurricane Irma, they instantly remember that photo.

I can share that photo anywhere around Jacksonville, and the chances are high that the person I am asking has seen that photo. Thats a wild statement to me, that it became iconic. I would show it to random strangers in my travels for several months afterwards, just curious if they had seen it. Most of the time, they had.

The popularity of it on facebook made all the follow up stories possible. I was a guest on the first broadcast of River City Live on WJXT Channel 4 after the storm, where I was able to share some of my photos, my experiences during Irma, and reach a wide mainstream audience besides social media. At the same time, I was being contacted by Resident Community News, Jacksonville Magazine, and Void magazine for publications of their own. The image appeared in local publications throughout Florida and beyond. A photo from that day made its way to a *National Geographic* photo assignment.

Within 2 days of Irma striking, I was back at Times-Union and printing up copies of "Life In The River" to be sold with 50% of the proceeds at the time going to Memorial Park Association. When I posted the photo online and gave my contact information on TV and elsewhere, I became flooded with emails of people wanting to buy prints. It was astounding to witness.

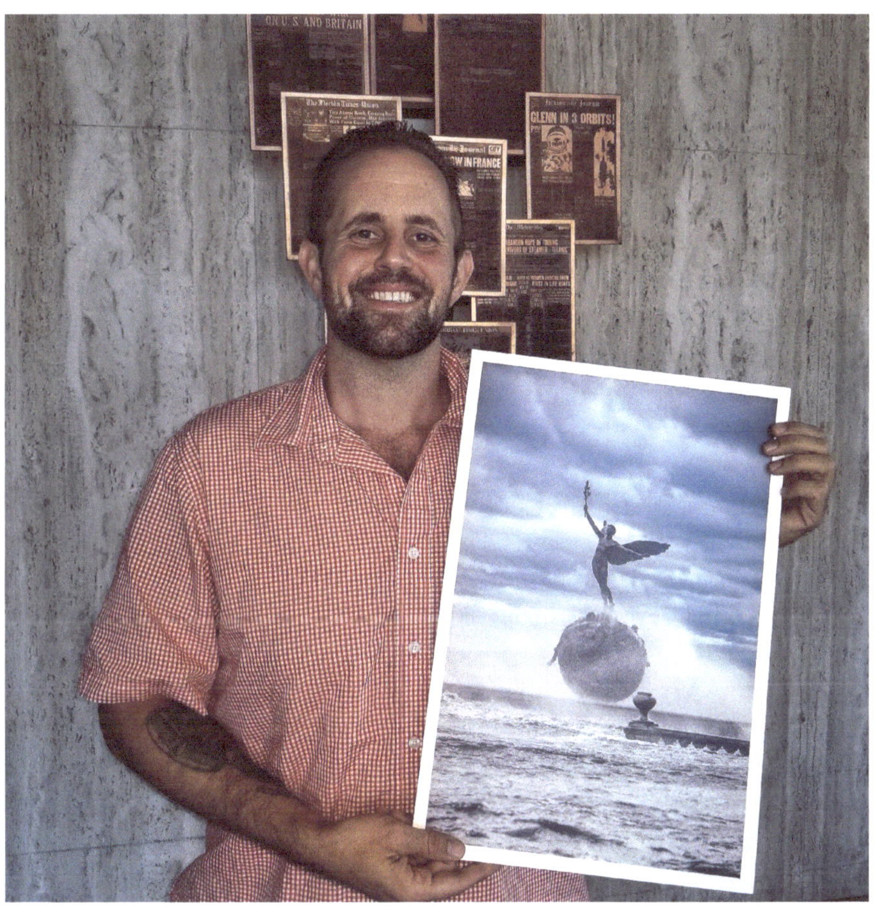

The photo brought its fair share of controversy though. Some people declared it was photoshopped and were trying to justify all sorts of ways to say it was. Generally, when I showed them the rest of the photo album from that day, they retracted their statements. Some people could not understand the angle I shot the photo from, so I have had to explain that numerous times. The balustrades that are present going towards the green space in the park confuse people.

There was a photographer who had his photos from Memorial Park stolen. They were used in ads fraudulently. People thought I had stolen this photographer's work, and were ready to come down to my first signing of prints at the 5 and dime theatre and protest. Fortunately they never did so, because I reached out to the photographer in question and he helped me out by telling the facebook group that had been formed to protest my signing that my photo was in fact not his photo.

I had began going to art walks earlier in 2017, and had met a man named Brooks Whalen of Local Goods Market. When this photo went everywhere, he volunteered not only to give his time and website expertise to have an online marketplace to sell the print, but he donated all his proceeds to Memorial Park! It was having this foundation and logistical help that really allowed me to fulfill the requests that were coming at me. But without having that basic foundation, I would have been lost and completely overwhelmed.

Eventually, the photo within the first year went on to be sold in homes as far away as Seattle, Los Angeles, North Dakota, Texas, New York City, Italy, Sweden, and many other locales. It is incredible to get that widespread recognition for my work, and goes to show you that through life's storms, good can come. Although many people still suffer from the effects of that storm, we can move past it. It did not defeat us. Everything works together for God's glory, and His plan for our lives is infinite. We cannot comprehend His infinite plan with our finite minds. The sales of "Life In The River" has lead to a wonderful partnership with Memorial Park Association, where over $12,000 in money and services has been donated to the Association 2 years up until this writing. This, coming from a man who was just getting out of prison a few years ago and starting a love for photography on his phone in a park he loves. It just goes to show you, that God is good! He has a plan, one that I could not have possibly envisioned for myself, but I am grateful for!

The stories of people I have heard from that photo, how they are connected to the park, always grab my attention. People have such a personal connection to this place. I have been blessed to photograph people who had photos taken there in the 1930s, now much older but still young at heart, in the same stance they were in originally in the park. I have grown as a person by appreciating the landscape architects who created the park originally, and their tie to other prominent parks throughout the country. It is something I never had thought of before my involvement with Memorial Park. For all this, I have grown as a person, and you can't put a price tag on that knowledge.

I notice that my photo resonates much more with people who have been to the park at some point in their lives. People in the international community think it is a cool photo, but they do not understand it like someone who has been there, or who grew up going to that park. Someone who has memories, much like I had made, in the park.

Photography began as a passion, and I feel for you to succeed at it, it has to always remain a passion. That doesn't mean that you can't do it as a job, but you have to truly love what you do, and sacrifice and go the extra mile. I suppose the same could be said for any other job that you love, but I never felt that way about something I could consider a career, before photography.

Since beginning this passion for photography, I have been blessed with multiple group and solo exhibits near and far. From the Karpeles Manuscript Museum in Springfield, to New York City to Madrid, Spain and Milan, Italy. It has been a great honor to be a part of these exhibits! As an artist, being

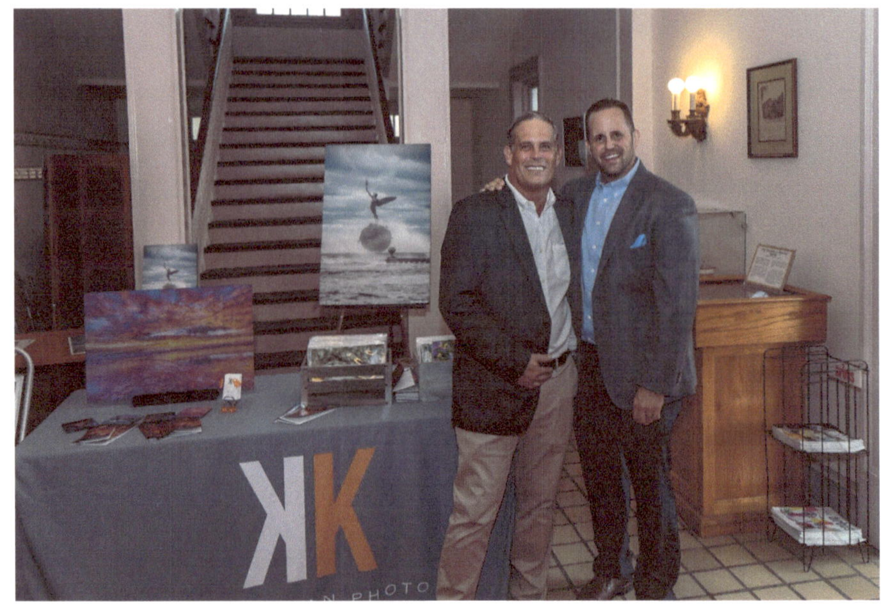

Art Patron and friend Bill Brim with Mark Krancer during the opening reception at the Karpeles Manuscript Museum, March 2019. Photo credit: Scott Dumaop

able to display your work is a great feeling. When others appreciate what you do, that positive reinforcement helps!

18. Jen

Around May 2016, over a year before Hurricane Irma, a co-worker tagged in a post on Facebook calling to artists at the Jacksonville International Airport. I laughed and said to myself, "Yeah right, the Haskell Gallery, good luck!" I did not know much about the art world but I knew Haskell was a major patron of the arts.

Eventually I figured that I'll never know unless I try. I filled out the application, submitted it and I heard nothing for months. I kind of forgot about it and figured I didn't have much of a chance anyway.

Then I received an email out of the blue saying, "Congratulations!"

My work was selected for the third quarter, "On City and Culture" exhibit in the Haskell Gallery! I was so excited and started planning how I was going to pull this off. Jen Jones is a genius in collaboration efforts and was my go-to person for questions. Her energy and willingness to bring the artist's and the airports vision together in such a powerful is truly inspiring.

Being accepted into the Haskell Gallery made me grow as an artist because it challenged me to create work that represented Jacksonville and the entire First Coast. That was a huge responsibility and I wanted to do it right. This was the validation I had been looking for from the world for a while. It was very nice and rewarding for me when others appreciated my passion for photography. I sold a few canvases before that time and had a few exhibits but nothing quite like this. The dedication to this exhibbit, and the space itself, was at the next level for me.

Being accepted gave me confidence to pursue photography further. I created my photography business, Kram Kran Photo,

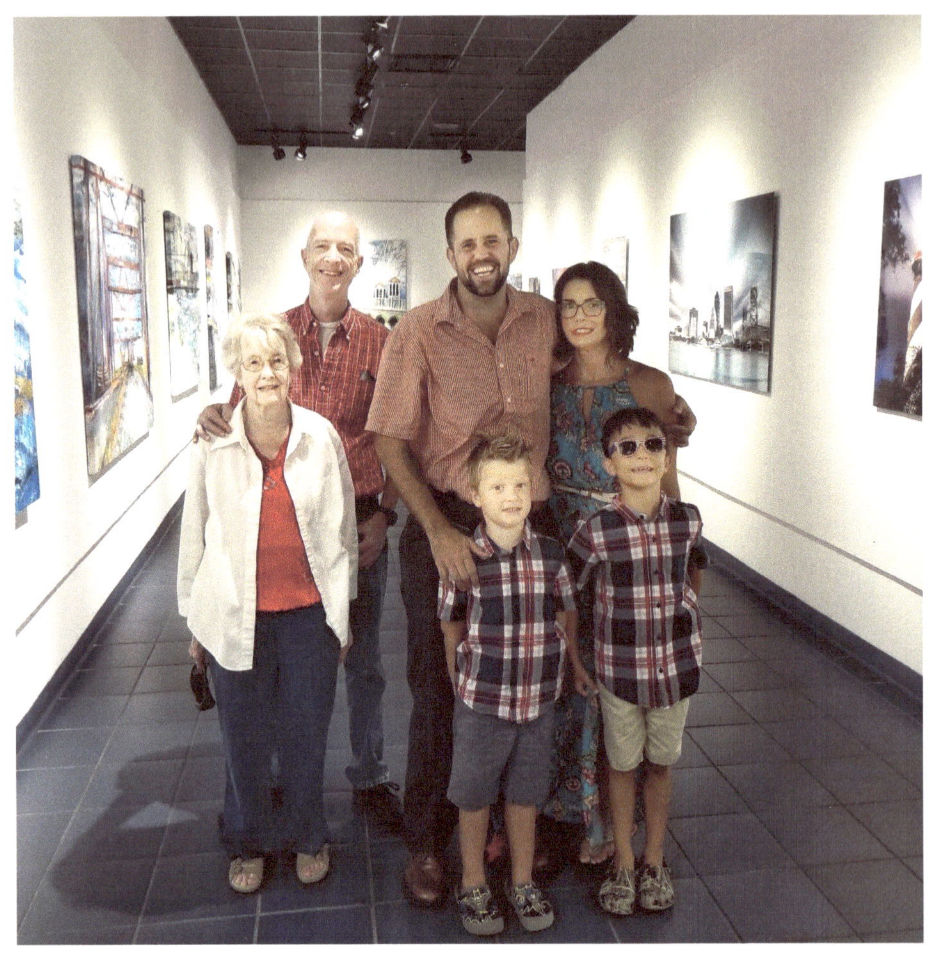

Celebrating the Haskell Gallery installation, July 2017. From left to right: Bob's mother Edith, Bob Tebbs, Mark Krancer, his stepson Logan Alverson, Kristin Krancer, and stepson Gavin Alverson.

a few months after being invited to show at the airport. I started pursuing downtown art walks and regional art fairs as well as becoming a freelance photographer for First Coast Magazine.

Jen not only supports the artists before their exhibit debuts but during it as well. We had an opening reception along with Marsha Glaziere, whom I shared the exhibit space with. The networking and appreciation of art that I felt there was tremendous and the reception lead to several sales.

When I took the photo of hurricane Irma, "Life In The River" I knew that I had to share it with Jen. She guided me through how to market, price, and strategize this photo to ensure its success. I was completely unprepared in this area and did not know what I was doing. I went from getting one business email a week to receiving over five hundred emails wanting to buy that print. I was so overwhelmed and with her guidance, along with a dedicated team of people, have sold hundreds of prints. This has blessed not only me but the Memorial Park Association recovery efforts. Jen allowed the flexibility to get this photo in my exhibit quickly as it became relevant overnight!

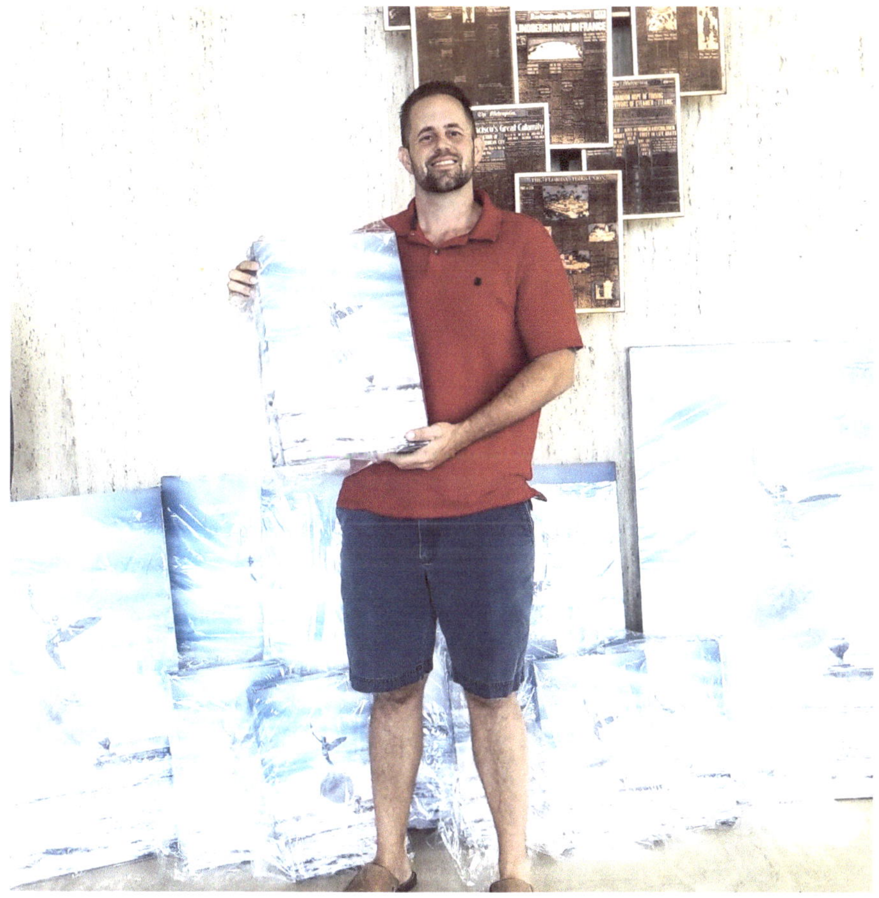

Mark with a new shipment of purchased canvas prints to sign, October 2017.

A few months after all that excitement, I had this to say about my experiences up to that point:

"Now that I am just over two weeks away from hearing the decision on whether the, "Life In The River" photo series will win a Pulitzer Prize in either the breaking news photography category or the feature photography category, I have no clue what will happen. No matter what, I know I have to at least try to win. I can honestly say I would have never even thought of a grand ambition if my passion for photography had not been recognized by Jen and the Jacksonville International Airports Arts Commission beforehand. No matter what stage you are in as an artist, the airport is there to help!"

I ultimately did not win the Pulitzer prize or even become a finalist. However that spirit of trying was exciting and I would gladly do it all over again! I have been truly blessed by Jen's friendship over the years.

My passion to go after many other arts related projects, which included bringing a permanent VIP club exhibit to the airport, having a print in the University of North Florida Special Collections department and donating pieces for charitable silent auction have all stemmed from her. She has encouraged me all along the way, because that is truly the kind of person she is!

19. Fire Flies with Kristin

A little over a month after taking "Life In The River", our wedding date arrived. It was sweet to have our wedding at the same church Kristin and I met at, being married by my father figure Steve Clifton. My short sighted economic concerns going into the marriage were lifted due to print sales and allowed me to focus on providing for the family in the ways I needed to.

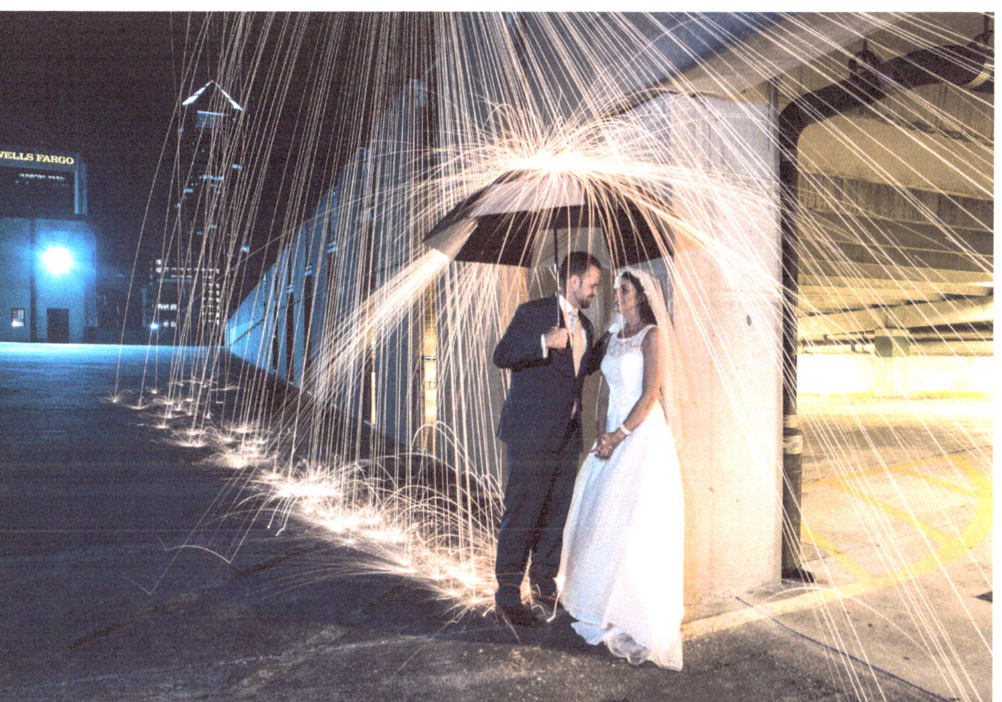

Mark and Kristin's wedding photo using steel wool photography, Photo Credit: Kevin Lind

We took a fun photo on the parking garage of First Baptist Church of Jacksonville, which I have attached in this book. The technique is called, "Steel Wool Spinning" and it goes something like this: take a piece of steel wool, fine grade (00 or finer), put it in a whisk. Then you attach the whisk to a rope, light it on fire and spin it around. It took several takes to get it right. We had to remain perfectly still as the steel wool was spinning above us. Some of these fiery sparks even burned through the umbrella and landed in Kristin's hair as she had her veil on. She knew the drill and remained perfectly still! That shot was the one that became our finished photo and hangs in our family room today. The best things about photography is when you have a vision and are able to bring it to life. With the help of our talented photographers Kevin Lind and Matt Bluejay we were able to accomplish our ideal photo for our wedding.

It was wonderful to have my dad and my buddy Lucas present at our wedding. They have been with me through thick and thin and they got to see my life come full circle. If Jesus can save a wretch like me then He can save anyone from bondage. Jesus alone broke the chains of addiction and sin in my life and He has paid a cost that I can never repay. His blood has washed my sins away and I am eternally grateful. As I write this book, there has been numerous times I have revisited chapters in my life and stories that remind me just how blessed I truly am.

Kristin and I have started married life together and we now live together with our boys where everyday moments can be cherished. I am a grateful man to be given this tremendous responsibility and opportunity. When I think of how far the Lord has brought me since the beginning of my relationship with Him I realize how truly blessed I am to be a productive member of a free society.

As time goes on I hear of more reports of friends from my old life who have passed away as victims of overdoses while many others still continue to revolve in and out of jail and addiction. I realize how easily that could have been me as I was well on my way to being part of that growing number of opiate deaths.

I was voted the Bold City Best's "Best Photographer" in 2018. This is an amazing validation for what I do and encouraged me to take a leap of being a full time photographer with Kristin's blessing.

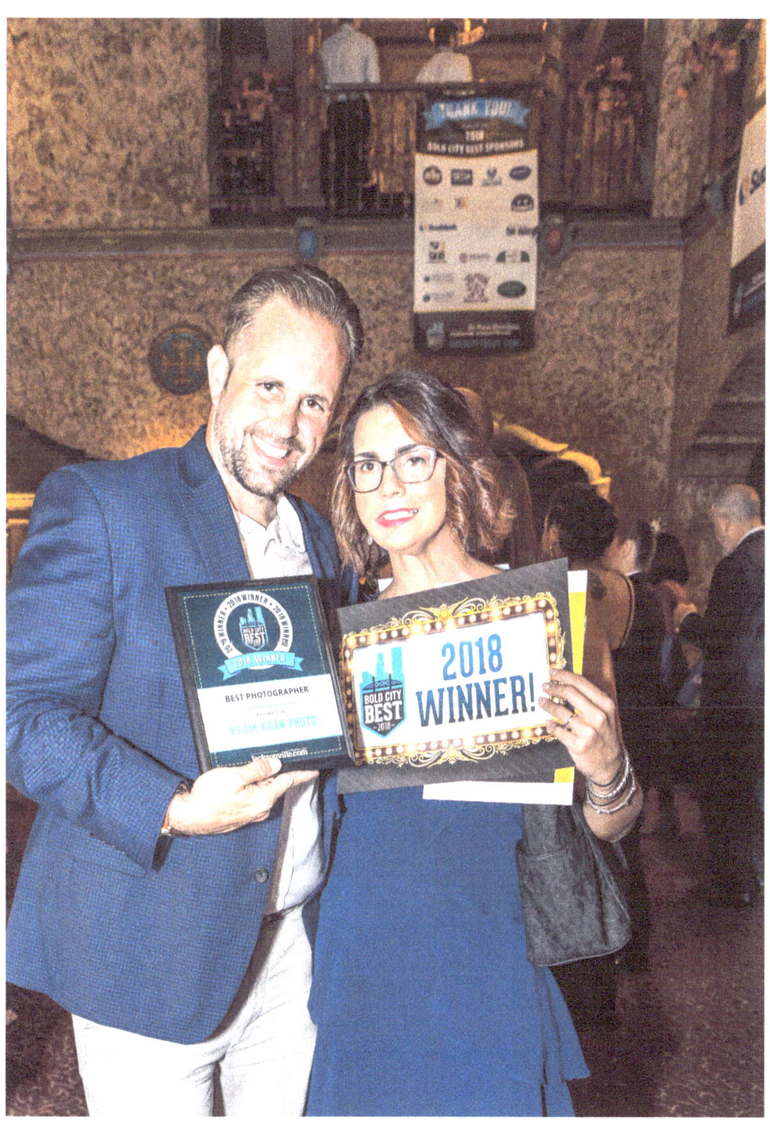

I have been blessed to pursue my love of photography on a full time basis now which supports me and my family. I love being a part of the many exciting ventures in Memorial Park, Jacksonville and beyond. I contribute in a visually creative way to many commercial, government, and non-profit organizations throughout the state of Florida. People judge me by the quality of work I produce and not by my past. Many of my prints hang on walls all over the world and I am blessed to get to capture many special moments. I explore old tunnels in the name of historic preservation, explore the sky at over eight thousand feet in the air, and plenty of opportunity in between!

I have just passed 7 years clean and sober for which I praise the Lord for every day! It is a great honor when I am asked to share my testimony with church groups, garden clubs, or people just getting out of prison and those still in prison. I can empathize with those men and women and hopefully they are encouraged by my story. I try not to embellish in any way but merely share what the Lord has done in my life. I have seen my wife, Kristin, get involved with prison ministry which warms my heart dearly. My aim in life is to let people know that the Lord has bigger plans for us that we can dream up for ourselves, that mistakes are not the end of the road, and that prisons and storms of life can be a place of transformation and inspiration to start a new path. The only true prison in this life is being apart from the Lord Jesus Christ.

My hope in this life is Christ alone.

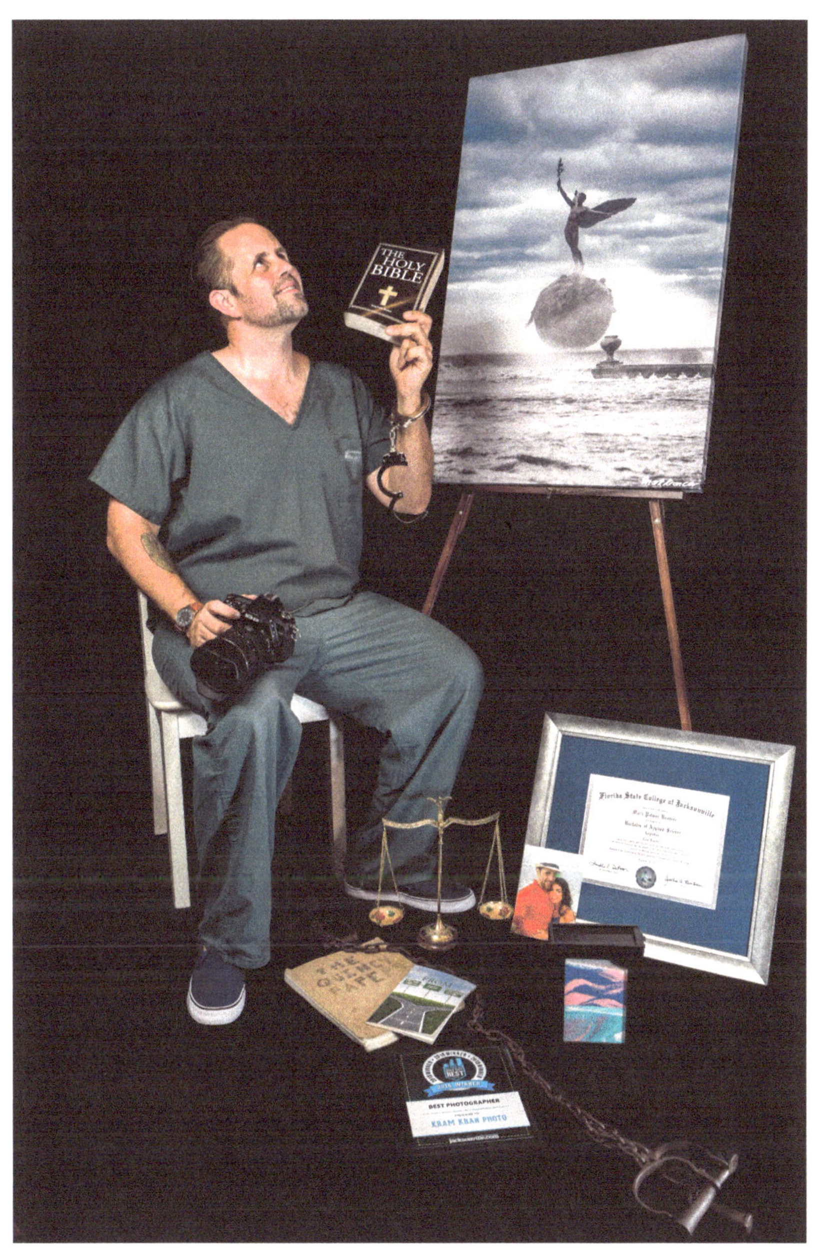

Mark's self portrait in the "more than a
DC number", project, 2019.

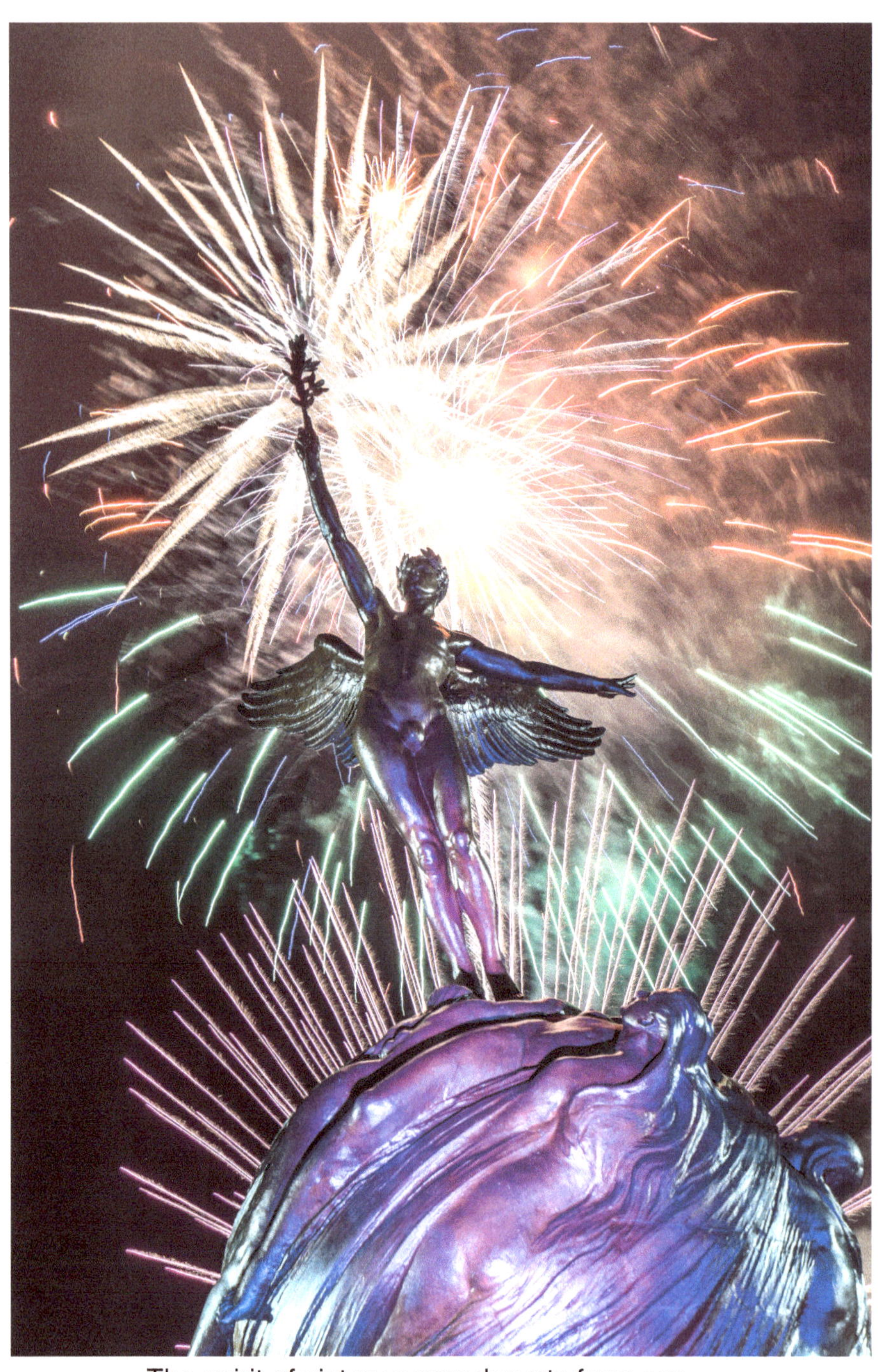

The spirit of victory never departs from our beloved Memorial Park, through all of Life's storms

Timeline

-1984 Born
-1985 Moved to Texas
-1996 Parents divorce
-1997 Moved to Sugarland, TX
-1997 Two week hiking trip to Philmont Boy Scout Ranch in New Mexico
-1998 Began high school
-1999 Start working at Everquest
-2001 Moved to Dallas, TX
-2001 Quit working at Everquest
-2002 Graduated from Lake Highlands HS
-2002 Dtarted at University of Houston
-2002 Received first DUI
-May 2003 Got kicked out of University of Houston
-2003 Moved to Melbourne, FL
-2003 Began school at Brevard Community College
-2003 Irwin Research, Carl
-April 2004 Mother dies
-2004 Meet Max
-April 2006 Received second DUI, cocaine charge
-2006 Start working at Fiserv
- 2007 Laccy committed suicide and started selling drugs again
- 2008 Bought house
- 2008 Began Oxycodone addiction
- 2009 Received third DUI (reduced to reckless driving)
- April 2010 Received fourth DUI
- June 2012 Gave my life to the Lord, but still an addict
- September 27, 2012 Sale of Oxycodone charge
- October 2012 Began working out
- January 2013 Transferred to Florida Department of Corrections
- Went to Quincy Correctional Institution
-August 2013 Transferred to the Bridge Theraputic Community
-January 5, 2014 Released from Prison

-January 5, 2014 Given shelter at Prisoners of Christ
-March 2014 Began work at the Florida Times-Union
-May 2014 Met Steve Clifton and began discipleship
-July 2014 Moved to riverside neighborhood
-September 2014 Began photographing on a cell phone on riverwalk
-April 2015 Acted in the First Baptist church's passion play
-April 2015 Met my love Kristin
-August 2015 First exhibit at Library
-April 2016 Regained driver's license
- May 2016 Exhibit at the Cool Moose Cafe
- July 4, 2016 Proposed to Kristin
- January 2017 Began as freelance photographer at the First Coast magazine
- May 2017 "Altered Objects" at downtown library
- July 2017 "On City and Culture" at Jacksonville Airport
- August 2017 Earned Bachelor degree in Logistics and Supply Chain management
- September 2017 the Five and Dime theatre Company exhibit
- September 2017 Digital display in "Kodak Moments" exhibit, Usagi Art Gallery, Brooklyn, NY
- October 2017 Married Kristin!!!!
- September 2018 Voted Bold City Best's "Best Photographer"
- November 2018 Quit the full time job for photography
- March 2019 Karpeles Manuscript Museum exhibit
- May 2019 JAX club permanent art installation, Jacksonville International Airport

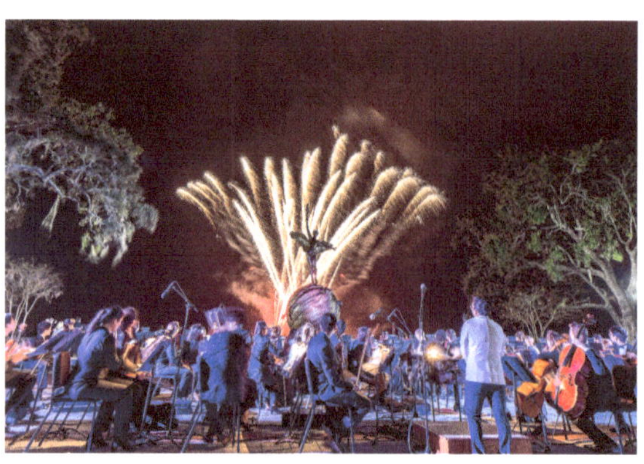

CITATION:

February 06, 2017. *Mass Incarceration Costs $182 Billion Every Year, Without Adding Much to Public Safety*
https://eji.org/news/mass-incarceration-costs-182-billion-annually

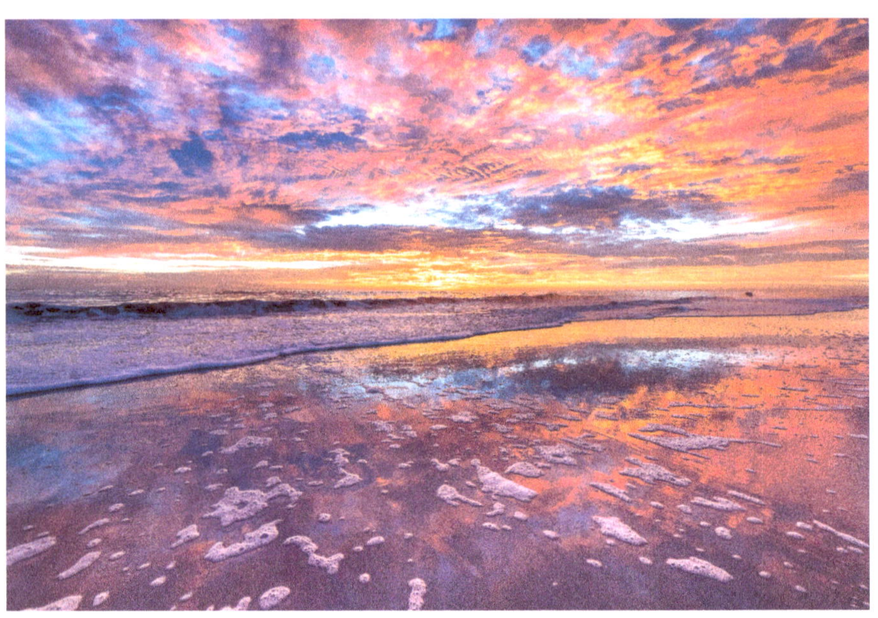

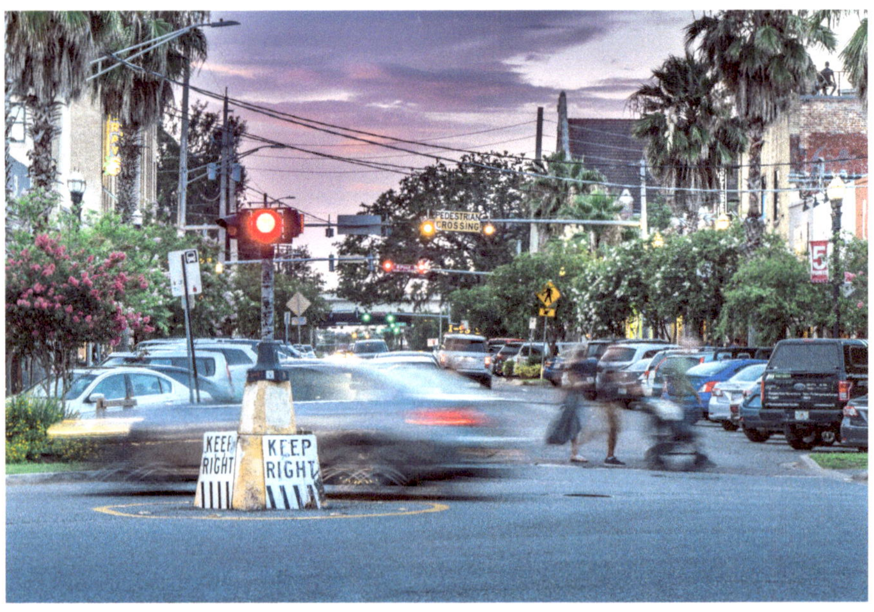
PEDESTRIAN
CROSSING
KEEP
RIGHT
KEEP
RIGHT

www.ingramcontent.com/pod-product-compliance
Lightning Source LLC
Chambersburg PA
CBHW041220050726
47599CB00001B/16